Praise for *Red Light, Green Light*

"Patterson weaves a heart-wrenching tale."

—Martin Hernandez, *LA Weekly*

"Erik Patterson may very well be the next great American playwright. His keen insight into the human condition comes alive in the second installment of his American Family Trilogy... You will come away uplifted and full of hope."

—Don Grigware, *NoHo LA*

"Patterson's play is a complex, non-linear affair... The work is an uplifting piece, peppered with marvelous speeches, economical writing, and lightning fast exchanges. I can't wait for the final installment in the trilogy."

—Matthew Breen, *OUT Magazine*

"Take an ordinary, screwed-up family—okay, maybe not so ordinary but definitely screwed up—and allow them to be honest with each other for the first time, and you have a powerful evening of love, American style. A mother researches every nuance of gay life (from sex toys to Matthew Shepard) in order to understand her son, a sister becomes Bjork to deal with abuse-trauma, a daughter/mother/lap dancer finally finds herself, a brother falls in love despite his tortured past. Every member of this extended family steals your heart as they daringly begin to recognize their own. Dark, funny, and searingly insightful, playwright Erik Patterson is on the road to great renown."

—Lee Bradley, *Flavorpill.net*

"With *Yellow Flesh/Alabaster Rose*, Erik Patterson emerged as a compelling new voice who could fashion strangely seductive drama and mine richly moving comedy from the deep domestic trauma of a broken family as it pieced itself back together... In his new sequel, *Red Light Green Light*, Patterson's complicated empathy for his flawed characters, as well as his disarming wit, are in full effect."

—Rob Kendt, *Los Angeles Times*

Red Light, Green Light

Plays by Erik Patterson

Tonseisha

Yellow Flesh / Alabaster Rose

Red Light, Green Light

He Asked For It

Sick

I Wanna Hold Your Hand

One of the Nice Ones

Handjob

Books by Erik Patterson

Pop Prompts: 200 Writing Prompts Inspired by Popular Music

Pop Prompts For Swifties: 99 Writing Prompts

Red Light, Green Light

by Erik Patterson

Camden High Street Books
2023

Print ISBN: 979-8-9878016-9-7
eBook ISBN: 979-8-9882250-1-0

Library of Congress Control Number: 2023907237

First Paperback Edition, May 2023

Copy editing by Sherry Angel
Cover image by Toa Heftiba

Printed in the United States of America
Los Angeles, CA
www.erikpatterson.org

"He sees alien people
and begins to understand
how alike they are to him.

He sees courage
and aspiration
and agony
and begins to understand himself.

He begins to feel himself a brother
in a race that is led by many dreams."

—Vachel Lindsay, poet, 1915

PRODUCTION HISTORY

Red Light, Green Light had its world premiere at Theatre of NOTE in Los Angeles on May 28, 2004. It was directed by Miguel Montalvo. The scenic design was by Jason Adams and Alicia Hoge, the lighting and sound design was by Robert Oriol, the costume design was by Ann Closs-Farley, the prop design was by Carolyn Hennesy, the production stage manager was Lauralea Oliver, and it was produced by David Bickford and Lisa Kenner. The cast was:

ELLIOT	Christopher Neiman
LITTLE B	Mandy Freund
BECKY	Jennifer Ann Evans
MOM	Sarah Lilly
ROSE	Rachel Kann
KRISTEN	Sofie Calderon
AVI	Phinneas Kiyomura
CALEB	Trevor H. Olsen
DAMIEN	Alan Loayza
KENNY	Stewart Skelton
RUTH	Judith Ann Levitt
BARRY	Brad C. Light
FRANK	Scott McKinley

After opening weekend, Phinneas Kiyomura took over the role of Elliot. Terry Tocantins joined the cast in Kiyomura's role.

The understudies were Dawn Greenidge (Kristen), Courtney Hoffman (Little B, Rose), Lauren Letherer (Mom), and Erik Patterson (Elliot, Avi.)

The production transferred to the Evidence Room Theatre on August 8, 2004 with Melanie Lora taking over the role of Little B and Mark McClain Wilson taking over the role of Kenny.

CHARACTERS

ELLIOT, thirty, a high school teacher.

LITTLE B, his sister, fifteen. Thinks she's Bjork, the Icelandic pop singer.

BECKY, their older sister, thirty-one. A stripper.

MOM, in her fifties, the mother of Elliot, Little B, and Becky.

ROSE, Becky's daughter, fifteen. Pregnant. Goth.

KRISTEN, Becky's girlfriend, in her thirties. A stripper.

AVI, twenty-five, Israeli. A student of philosophy.

CALEB, thirties. A professional clown.

DAMIEN DEMETER, Rose's ex-boyfriend, sixteen. Also a Goth.

KENNY, a man in his forties.

RUTH, mother of Caleb, in her sixties. A housewife.

BARRY, a hustler, in his thirties.

FRANK, a man in his forties.

TIME AND PLACE

It is 2004.

There are many locations. They can be suggested. Don't bother with big set pieces that require complicated transitions. We should move from one scene to the next as fluidly as possible.

PROLOGUE

In darkness, we hear the wail of a siren
approaching. The siren's scream grows
louder until it's almost unbearable.

Suddenly, the sound is sucked away, as if
into a vacuum, and silence fills the air.
Then: the steady beat of a heart monitor,
tick tick ticking like a metronome.

Lights up on Becky, alone, in a strip club
cubicle.

BECKY (*to the audience*): Hi. Hello. Hi.
   I'm sorry: I haven't talked about this much, so it might come out
   awkward. I'm just trying to make sense, and sometimes it's hard
   to find the right words. My brother—

> *Lights up on Elliot, unconscious in a*
> *hospital bed. Becky looks at him.*

My brother isn't doing well. Jesus, my brother. I don't understand
how this happened.

> *Lights fade out on Elliot.*

1

The thing is, just when you think you've gotten control of—

a handle on—

your life...

When you think you've gotten...

I'm sorry. I can't go on. I think I'm gonna throw up. You came to see me work. All right, okay, all right. Focus, Becky, focus.

> *She snaps her fingers. The sound of the heart monitor morphs into the throbbing base beat of the strip club. Becky makes provocative poses: slowly, steadily, deliberately.*

Hi, handsome. What's your name? Ever been here before? You have, I can tell. Don't be shy. I can tell by the way you tilted your head, just a hair, and then you kind of blushed a little bit in your neck. Don't be ashamed. It's okay. No one has to know. Just you and me.

> *She stops posing. To herself.*

This isn't working.

> *She snaps her fingers. The base beat cuts out.*

I don't know how to talk to guys anymore. Ever since I fell in love, I don't know how to talk to them. The last time I even fucked a guy was the night I met Kristen. That was six months ago.

She snaps again and suddenly it's six months earlier. Frank enters the cubicle. Becky glances at him, quickly takes him in.

FRANK: I'm Frank.
BECKY: Hi, Frank.
FRANK: What's your name?
BECKY: Hunter.
FRANK: I was wondering if...
BECKY: What?
FRANK: If instead of just dancing, if you could...if we...if I...
BECKY: Spit it out, Frank.
FRANK: If I could...hold you?
BECKY: You wanna hold me, Frank?
FRANK: Yeah.
BECKY: "Holding me" is gonna cost you more than thirty dollars.
FRANK: Okay.

He opens his wallet, hands Becky all his cash. He sits, undoes his pants.

3

Becky hands him a condom, straddles him as he puts it on. They start fucking. She turns her head away from Frank and resumes her conversation with the audience.

(Note: When she talks to the audience, she's back in the present. Frank is barely a memory. It's as if he's not there.)

BECKY (*to the audience*): Last night, I was at the hospital with—

Lights up on Elliot in the hospital bed again. Mom, Little B, and Kristen sit at his side, waiting for some sort of sign.

—my mother, my sister, and my girlfriend.

And I was just sitting there, thinking:

'He's not gonna make it. He's not gonna make it.'

The thought kept running through my head: 'He's not gonna make it.'

I almost had to slap myself because I believe in positive thinking.

And I believe that when you put a thought out there it can come true.

And I believe I might be feeding you a whole lot of bullshit right now.

Just stop. He's gonna make it.

Okay, okay, okay, okay, it's okay. okay. Okay.

Lights fade out on the hospital room.
Becky continues to fuck Frank.

FRANK: Do you believe in love?

The sound of his voice draws her
attention back to him.

BECKY: Sure.

FRANK: Have you ever been in love?

BECKY: All the time.

FRANK: Stop that.

BECKY: Stop what?

FRANK: Saying what you think I want to hear. Have you? Have you
ever been in love?

BECKY: Shut up, Frank. I want you to relax and just shut up.

She continues to fuck him, but turns her
attention back to the audience.

BECKY (*to the audience*): I just became a grandmother. I know you
think that's impossible: I'm 31 years old. You think I'm barely
old enough to be a mother, let alone a grandmother, but my

daughter Rose and I, we're making it work. My daughter Rose—

Lights come up on Rose and Damien Demeter, making out feverishly in one of the linoleum-tiled hallways of Chatsworth High School. They're both dressed from head-to-toe in black.

There she is. Before she was pregnant. Before she was including me in her life. Before the thing happened. The thing that happened to my brother.

Lights fade out on Rose and Damien.

Becky starts to fake an orgasm for Frank, while continuing to talk to us.

I'm trying to get out of this place. To get me and my girlfriend out. Because we're in love. And it's just time, you know? I want out, I need out, it's just that I've been saying that for fifteen years, you know? Hearing girls say that for fifteen years. And it's tough.

Frank starts to moan.

FRANK: Ohhh...I'm gonna...

*Becky stops fucking him. She finishes him
off with her hand.*

*As Frank buttons up his pants, puts
himself back together, Becky steps away
from him to finish her conversation with
the audience.*

BECKY (*to the audience*): The thing is, just when you think you've
gotten control of—
a handle on—
your life...something will happen.
Like what happened to my brother.
A random, senseless, unspeakable thing.
And then you'll realize that you don't have control
and you don't have a handle
and then your whole world will begin to unravel.
Wait.
I'm trying to test out my whole positive thinking theory, so let me
rephrase that:
Maybe you'll realize that you don't have control
and you don't have a handle
and then maybe it'll make you stronger.
FRANK: I'm sorry that was so—
BECKY (*to Frank again*): It was perfect.

7

Beat.

You have a gorgeous cock, Frank.

No one's ever said that to him before.

FRANK: Thanks.

Frank gets up to go.

FRANK: That was really…

He decides not to finish the thought.

You know, I'm not just some loser guy.
BECKY: I didn't say you were.
FRANK: I used to have a family. I have a kid.
BECKY: You do?
FRANK: Yeah, but I'm not very good at it. I don't know how to talk to him.
BECKY: You just talk.
FRANK: I'm bad at it. He lives with his mom, I don't really see him. Okay, well…

He starts to go. Becky stops him.

8

BECKY: You know, Frank?

FRANK: Yeah?

BECKY: I do believe in love. I have a kid too. And I love her.

FRANK: Yeah.

BECKY: You know, you should try to see your son. You should try to see him and talk to him.

FRANK: Yeah, I will. Okay.

BECKY: Bye, Frank.

FRANK: Thanks.

> *Frank exits. Becky leans back in her chair.*

> *After a beat, Kristen pokes her head into the cubicle.*

KRISTEN: Excuse me?

BECKY: Yeah?

KRISTEN: Hi, I'm Kristen.

BECKY: Hi Kristen. Nice to meet you.

KRISTEN: I saw you dancing out there. You're really good.

BECKY: Thanks.

KRISTEN: And I was wondering if I could get a lap dance?

BECKY: Let's hit it.

Becky snaps her fingers, a dance groove
starts playing, and the lap dance begins.

Lights stay on Becky and Kristen, as they
continue to dance, slowly, tenderly.

Lights up on Kenny.

He talks to the audience, but is aware of
the two women dancing.

KENNY: Last night, I wasn't in the mood, right?
   I just—
   Wasn't. In. The mood.
   It's like: sometimes I feel like my life's falling apart
   and when things get to be too much,
   something's gotta give, right?
   Something's gotta give.
   My life is for shit right now, right?
   Like, for instance—
   (and this is just one of the reasons)
   —my cousin Albert:
   —a really good guy;
   a really good, decent guy—
   he died recently, right?
   And his death was, like, this really fluke thing. Like:

One day he was fine,

and then the next day he had a sore throat,

and then the sore throat wouldn't go away—

but he wasn't worried about it because it was just a

fuckingsorethroat—

and then all of a sudden he was dead.

Just like that.

Poof.

Beat.

Freaky thing, right?

Gets worse...

Turns out he had meningitis,

which they discovered, like, two hours before he died.

I don't even know what the fuck meningitis is, really.

I mean, I'm not an idiot,

but I didn't know it was something

that was so bad for you

you're supposed to be afraid of getting it, suddenly, and then

being dead two hours later.

What the fuck is that, right?

It just makes me so mad.

It's not like Albert smoked all his life

and then got lung cancer, or:

ate bacon every morning and then had a heart attack, or:

like he was one of those people who...

(trailing off)

One of those...
you know...
Jesus.
My head's spinning right now, just thinking about it, right?
My head's...spinning.
How a person can be here one minute and then,
fucking dead.
But you can't go around thinking about shit like that all the time,
because, like I said before: it's gonna weigh you down,
and then it's gonna break you,
and then you're
nothing,
you know,
unless you let it go.
You just gotta let it go.
But, see—
last night, I was walking home,
walking through my neighborhood,
and I just wasn't in the mood for anyone
to lay their crap on me.
I was thinking about Albert,
and how harsh

and cruel

and unforgiving

life can suddenly become.

Because when a man as good

and decent

as my cousin Albert...

When a man like that suddenly dies of a stupid thing like

meningitis,

you start to think about the people who should have fucking died

instead of him.

You start to think about the people out there we'd be better off

without.

The people we'd be better off not knowing.

Beat.

And you start to think that there are a lot of people out there

who could use a good

fuckingspinalcordinfection,

if you know what I mean.

Just to wake.

Them.

Up.

Lights shift.

An apartment complex BBQ.

Kenny is serving up some food for himself. Elliot stands behind him, an empty paper plate in his hand.

ELLIOT: Are you gonna take that?

KENNY: You want it?

ELLIOT: Ted's cooking more. If you want it, I can wait.

KENNY: No, have it.

ELLIOT: Thanks.

Kenny shrugs. Elliot serves himself the last piece of chicken.

ELLIOT: I don't think we've ever met. I'm Elliot.

KENNY: Kenny.

ELLIOT: What apartment are you in?

KENNY: I don't live here. I'm just a friend of Ted's.

ELLIOT: I don't really know Ted.

Kenny looks for Ted. Is the chicken ready yet?

ELLIOT: So, where do you live?

KENNY: Four-one-one.

14

ELLIOT: Is that some sort of joke about "information" that I don't—

KENNY: No, I live down the street.

ELLIOT: Oh, that's your—

KENNY: Four-one-one.

ELLIOT: Address.

KENNY: Right.

ELLIOT: I get it now.

Awkward.

ELLIOT: How long have you been here? I mean the neighborhood, not
    the barbecue.

KENNY: Forty-two years—

ELLIOT: Wow.

KENNY: Give or take a few. My mom and dad died my first year
    away at school. I came back so we wouldn't lose the place.

ELLIOT: I'm sorry about your parents.

Kenny looks at Elliot's plate. He's
getting annoyed.

ELLIOT: Do you have any siblings?

KENNY: What?

ELLIOT: Brothers or sisters?

KENNY: I know what they are.

ELLIOT: Do you have any? Or is it just—

KENNY: Yeah.

ELLIOT: —you?

KENNY: Four brothers.

ELLIOT: Where do you fall?

KENNY: I'm the youngest.

ELLIOT: I'm the middle of three. Two sisters.

KENNY: You're not eating your chicken.

ELLIOT: I'm sorry?

KENNY: You haven't touched it.

ELLIOT: No.

KENNY: It's just that you insisted on having the last piece—

ELLIOT: I didn't insist—

KENNY: And you haven't...If you weren't going to eat it right away, you could've waited for the next batch.

ELLIOT: You want it?

KENNY: It's on your plate. You've touched it.

ELLIOT: I haven't eaten it.

KENNY: You've touched it with your fingers.

ELLIOT: I haven't.

To prove it, he puts the plate down.

KENNY: It's cold now.

ELLIOT: I'm sure there'll be more any second.

KENNY: That's not the point. I've been neglecting my girlfriend.

ELLIOT: I'm sorry. I—

KENNY: So I'll be going.

ELLIOT: It was nice to meet you.

> *Kenny exits. Elliot doesn't know what to do. He stands there, awkward. Another man, Barry, approaches the table for some food. He glances at Elliot, then gives a smile of recognition.*

BARRY: Hi. How are you?

> *Elliot looks embarrassed. Suddenly, even more awkward than before. He smiles back, weakly.*

> *Lights shift.*

ACT ONE

SCENE ONE

Living Room. Rose's baby shower. Becky, Kristen, Little B, and Mom surround Rose, who is seven-months pregnant. She looks ready to burst.

Mom hands her a large box.

MOM: It's from me.

ROSE (*shaking the box, joking*): I think it's underwear.

LITTLE B: It's shoes!

MOM: Hey!

LITTLE B: What?

MOM: You just told her.

LITTLE B: I got excited.

MOM: Little B helped me pick.

LITTLE B: Her boyfriend was there too.

ROSE: It's too big for shoes.

BECKY: Mom, you have a boyfriend?

MOM: Well, we haven't defined it yet, but possibly.

BECKY: I want details.

MOM: Later. This is Rose's day. Rose, open your present.

Rose opens the box, peers inside.

ROSE: Oh my God.

Rose pulls out a pair of baby boots.

KRISTEN: They're adorable.
LITTLE B: Aren't they?

Rose pulls out another pair, and another, and another...

MOM: Do you like them?
ROSE: Yeah.

    Thank you, Grandma.
BECKY: Rose, honey, are you okay?
MOM: The shoes were supposed to make you happy.
ROSE: They did.
MOM: But you look like you're going to cry.
ROSE: I am. Gonna cry. Happy. All of it. I'm just kind of emotional
    right now. There's so much to think about, to worry about. It's
    like...I get caught up in the thought of: little shoes, and little
    bottles, and little toys, and then all of these other little things. But
    it's more than just things, you know? Like, I look at these shoes
    and I start to think about the feet that are gonna be in these shoes.
    Little feet. Boy feet. Little boy feet attached to little boy legs

attached to little boy...boy. It's just kind of crazy because he seems so small and vulnerable and I haven't even had him yet—I mean, if I'm neurotic now, imagine how crazy I'm gonna be after he's born. Because right now I know exactly where he is, it's like: my uterus is the safest place he could be and even knowing that, there could still be complications inside of me. You never know. Anything could happen. So then I think to myself, "just get through these nine months, just keep him as safe as you possibly can now so that in a few months you can see him wear these shoes. And after that, you can take it from there and worry about the next little thing." But then I backtrack and start to wonder what it's gonna feel like to be in labor—and I know that's gonna be hard—it's gonna hurt, right?—but no matter how hard the labor is, everything after that's gonna be so much harder, you know? Because once he's come out of here and entered the world, then what? I'm gonna have this fragile little boy who's got a lot of little shoes. So maybe his feet will be protected, you know, safe from glass and rocks and, I don't know, little bugs or whatever else might attack his feet from the ground...but then what? What's gonna protect my little boy from everything else? From the rest of the world? It's just overwhelming and I get kind of obsessive thinking about all the possibilities of life and when I start fixating, then I have to stop myself, take a deep breath, and not think about shoes.

MOM: Get used to it.

ROSE: Why?

MOM: You have a lifetime of worry ahead of you. Now...open
    another present!

LITTLE B: Open mine.

*Little B hands Rose a small square-
shaped gift.*

BECKY: Looks like a CD.

ROSE: It's underwear, right?

LITTLE B: I can't tell you. Just open it.

ROSE: B, is this for the baby or for me? Because my birthday isn't
    until next week.

LITTLE B: It's for the baby, I promise.

KRISTEN: Are we doing birthdays today, too?

BECKY: No, just the shower.

MOM: We're doing birthdays next weekend. Open Little B's present!

Rose opens the present: Vespertine *by
Bjork.*

ROSE: Guess who?

LITTLE B: It is for the baby, see. It's my collection of lullabies, which
    you can play when he won't stop crying at night. You can let his
    Great Aunt Bjork sing him to sleep. It's not as good as the real
    thing, but I can't be over at your house all the time.

ROSE: Thanks, B.

LITTLE B: You could even start playing it for him now, if he kicks a lot. I read that listening to music in the womb makes a child smarter.

ROSE: Okay, I'll do that.

LITTLE B: I bought it with my own money. From my wages.

BECKY: Oh, that's right, you started your job, B. How is it?

LITTLE B (*to the tune of "Pagan Poetry" from* Vespertine): "I love it. I love it. I love it. I love it."

MOM: Where's Elliot. Why isn't he here yet?

ROSE: He said to go ahead without him. He'll be here late.

MOM: Then what do you want to open next?

KRISTEN: Wait, Rose—

ROSE: Yeah?

KRISTEN: You have an eyelash on your cheek.

> *She scoops it up with her finger and then presents it to Rose.*

BECKY: Make a wish...

LITTLE B: Wish for something amazing.

ROSE: Okay.

> *She closes her eyes, makes a wish, and blows.*

> *Lights shift.*

SCENE TWO

We're inside Heaven, a nightclub.

Loud thumping techno music pumps through speakers. Red and blue lights pulse.

Mom stands on the edge of the dance floor, a beer in her hand. A young man, Avi, approaches her.

AVI: Hi.

Rose smiles at the young man. She tries to say something, then gets embarrassed and doesn't say it, then looks away from him.

AVI: Wanna dance?

Rose looks at him, smiles, looks away.

AVI: Excuse me?
MOM: Yes?
AVI: Would you like to dance?

23

MOM: Are you talking to me?

AVI: Yeah.

MOM: Okay.

> *He starts to dance to the music. She just stands there and looks at him.*

MOM: I don't know how to dance to this music.

AVI: You just move.

> *He demonstrates. She tries to follow him.*

AVI: You're doing good.

MOM: What's your name?

AVI: Avi.

MOM: I'm Rose.

AVI: It figures.

MOM: What figures?

AVI: You're so gorgeous, it figures you'd have a name like "Rose."

MOM (*launching in*): I hope this isn't too forward.

AVI: Okay...

MOM: But I need to know if you've ever had an LTR?

AVI: What's that?

MOM: A Long Term Relationship. With a man.

AVI: What?

MOM: I won't judge you if you haven't, I just want to know.

AVI: No…My last relationship was with a woman. Named Eternity. Seriously.

MOM: A woman named Eternity?

AVI: We only lasted two years. Oh, God, that's a bad joke. Remind me to stop making that joke.

MOM: Avi?

AVI: What?

MOM: Aren't we in a gay club?

AVI: Well, it is kind of lame, but I wouldn't go that far.

MOM: You're not gay?

AVI: Sorry.

MOM: I feel incredibly stupid right now.

AVI: Do you mind explaining?

MOM: I thought this was a gay club.

AVI: I told you, it's really not that bad.

MOM: Would you stop making that joke?

AVI: I'm sorry. Seriously, though, Heaven's only gay on Fridays and Saturdays. It's mixed during the week.

MOM (*sudden realization*): Oh my God.

AVI: Is something wrong? Did I say something—

MOM: I just realized that you've been hitting on me.

AVI: Well, I've been trying to.

MOM: I've never been called 'gorgeous' before. Pretty, yes. But gorgeous...

AVI: You are.

MOM: You're really very sweet. I'm sorry you're not gay.

AVI: Why do you want me to be gay? What's your fixation?

MOM: I wanted to set you up with my son.

AVI: I can honestly say that I've never met anyone like you in my entire life. So you wanted to set me up with your son, eh?

MOM: Yeah, he's probably a little older than you. How old are you?

AVI: Twenty-five.

MOM: Oh, boy.

Beat.

Anyway, he's my only son. I want him to be happy. You understand, don't you?

AVI: Sure. But what were you going to do? I mean, if I was gay. I'm curious. What were you gonna do?

MOM: Get your number. Give it to Elliot. I don't know. I hadn't thought things through that far. I'm crazy, I know.

AVI: No—

MOM: I'm just a crazy mother.

AVI: No, you're not. Are you married?

MOM: Oh, no.

AVI: Single?

MOM: Widow.

AVI: I'm sorry.

MOM: No, no, it's...

Beat.

I'm happy.

AVI: Have you...since he passed away, have you—

MOM: Had an LTR?

AVI: Yeah.

MOM: No. Well, I've had the "R" part, but not the "L" or the "T."

AVI: Okay, so, I know that you're looking to fix someone up with your son. And I think that's great. Really. I mean, the thought of my mom going to a bar looking for the woman of my dreams kind of freaks me out...but another mom doing it...you doing it...Well, that just makes you even more interesting than I thought you'd be when I first saw you standing alone over here. It makes you really charming. And I was wondering—

MOM: You're asking me out.

AVI: Well, I've been trying to.

MOM: I'd love to.

Lights shift.

SCENE THREE

Little B and Elliot sit at their breakfast table. She eats cereal. They're both reading the newspaper.

After a moment:

LITTLE B: Elliot?

ELLIOT: What, B?

LITTLE B: I've been thinking lately and I'm worried.

ELLIOT: About what, B?

LITTLE B: I don't know, that's the thing.

ELLIOT: You don't have to worry about anything.

LITTLE B: I know. But you know how "my instinctiveness is 50 times more wise than my head?"

ELLIOT: Okay.

LITTLE B: Well, "my instinct is going, 'yeah, go, go, go!' and my head is going, 'This is the most ridiculous thing you could ever do in your life. It's so stupid.'" So I don't know what to do.

ELLIOT: What's stupid?

LITTLE B: I want a job.

ELLIOT: Okay. How about you start doing your own laundry and I'll raise your allowance two dollars?

LITTLE B: No. I want a real job. In the world.

ELLIOT: You're fifteen. You should be focusing on your homework, not getting a job.

LITTLE B: "I think I'm half fifteen-years-old and the other half of me is 50. But the side of me that's 50 is very private."

ELLIOT: Yeah, well, you gotta show a little more of that 50-year-old before I let you out in the world like that. It's a big step, B.

LITTLE B (*desperate*): Please.

ELLIOT: Why do you want it so badly?

LITTLE B: I just feel like there has to be something more than just this. It's fine to have concerts and everything. But all of a sudden, I feel like I need something more, just to feel normal. Because I don't live a normal life.

ELLIOT: You don't want a normal life.

LITTLE B: I do.

ELLIOT: You're a pop star.

LITTLE B: "I don't know about the star thing, because I did a record in Iceland when I was 11—"

ELLIOT: I know, I know.

LITTLE B: "—which became quite popular, and people recognized me in the street, but at the same time Reykjavik is such a small society that they always put you in your place, you know? I mean, you can never be a star in Iceland because people will always see you on the bus or catch you farting in a shop or walking down Main Street."

ELLIOT: Will they, now?

LITTLE B: Yes. "So you can never get this distance of being a star. And even today when I go to Iceland and a taxi-driver picks me up, he's like 'Oh, don't you for one minute pretend you're any more important than me—I met your grandmother in the swimming pool the other day and she says you never call her.' So they put you in your place. I've been used to it."

ELLIOT: But do you really want a job?

LITTLE B: Yes. I read this thing and it made me quite scared.

ELLIOT: What was it?

LITTLE B: About this man who wanted to do this really bad thing to her.

ELLIOT: Her who?

LITTLE B: I mean, me.

ELLIOT: It was an article?

LITTLE B: In *Rolling Stone*.

ELLIOT: You know, B...

LITTLE B: What?

ELLIOT: When bad things happen to her, you don't have to take them on if you don't want to. You have permission to just believe the good things.

LITTLE B: "There's nothing I can do about it, really. I just find it sad that people get in that kind of state, you know?"

ELLIOT: I know.

LITTLE B: The man's dead, anyway.

ELLIOT: You know, B...

LITTLE B: What?

ELLIOT: Dad's dead too.

LITTLE B: I know.

ELLIOT: He's gone. None of that's ever gonna happen again. So if you ever want me to call you Rebecca again, you should let me know. I'm not pushing you. But I want you to know that you're safe here.

Beat. She looks away from him.

ELLIOT: I just want you to be happy.

LITTLE B: A job would make me happy.

ELLIOT: Okay.

LITTLE B: Really?

ELLIOT: Yeah, okay, yeah. You know what job you'd want?

LITTLE B: I want to help kids believe in magic.

Lights shift.

SCENE FOUR

A man in full clown garb—face, wig, suit and shoes—sits at a desk. Elliot and Little B enter.

ELLIOT: Hi. Hello. Hi, um, are you—. Um.

CALEB: Can I help you?

ELLIOT: Do you work here?

CALEB: Do I look like I work here?

ELLIOT: Right, dumb question. I'm sorry, could we—. Is there a manager we could talk to?

CALEB: What do you wanna talk about?

ELLIOT: A job—we're looking for a job.

CALEB: Both of you?

ELLIOT: Yeah. I mean, no. I mean, we're both looking, but she's the one—. I mean, the job would be for her.

CALEB: Who's she?

ELLIOT: She's my sister.

LITTLE B: He's my brother.

ELLIOT: I'm her legal guardian.

LITTLE B: His name is Elliot.

ELLIOT: And she's Little B.

LITTLE B: You can call me Bjork.

CALEB: Okay, Bjork, how old are you?

LITTLE B: I'm—

ELLIOT: She's fifteen.

CALEB: So she doesn't have a driver's license?

ELLIOT: Not quite.

LITTLE B (*annoyed*): Elliot.

(*to Caleb*)

I'm learning. I have my permit.

CALEB: The job requires a driver's license.

ELLIOT: I don't mind being her chauffeur. I'm a teacher, so my weekends are free, and I assume she'd be working on the weekends.

LITTLE B (*to Elliot*): Elliot, do you mind? I appreciate the help, but this is my job interview. Could you please let me do the talking?

ELLIOT (*taken aback*): Sorry. Go ahead.

LITTLE B (*to Caleb*): As I was saying, I have my permit, and my brother has graciously offered to drive me to birthday parties until I get my license, so please don't view my age as a hindrance.

CALEB: All right then, I won't.

LITTLE B: Now—before we go any further: you haven't told me your name.

CALEB: It's Bobo.

LITTLE B: Hello, Bobo. Nice to meet you.

CALEB: Okay, that was a joke. My name's actually Caleb. And yours actually is...?

LITTLE B: I told you, you can call me Bjork.

CALEB: It's actually Bjork. Okay. I never heard of an American named Bjork.

LITTLE B: You never heard of me?

CALEB: She's one of my favorite singers, you know.

LITTLE B: I am?

Caleb looks at her. Who IS this girl?

CALEB: Sure.

LITTLE B: Thank you very very much.

CALEB: If I hire you, am I gonna have to worry about all of the kids asking for your autograph?

LITTLE B: Well, I suppose if it's part of the job. But really "how on earth am I supposed to change people's lives if I'm just scribbling my name on a paper card?"

CALEB: Okay, then, Bjork, let me ask you this: Do you ever regret the breakup of the Sugarcubes?

LITTLE B: No.

Caleb's about to get on with the interview, but then—

"It was the way it was just meant to be. Six years after we started Bad Taste Records, we formed the Sugarcubes as a joke. Well, not exactly a joke, but there were three poets who were actually in the writers union in Iceland in the Sugarcubes, and we were trying to change things—big time—which I think we actually did a little bit. We were trying to stop narrow-mindedness. I am very proud of that period in my life. But it is very important to stop things when they are finished. And it just wasn't right for us to get into a situation where you're having one of the most promising writers in Iceland playing bass and he hadn't written one thing in four years because he was doing a sound check in Texas. As much as intellectually it was very very stimulating to hang out with poets and authors, musically it just wasn't challenging anymore for me. I had just become a little more mature and I was craving and hungry to meet people who felt the same way about music as I did."

CALEB: I was joking.

She just looks at him.

CALEB: Were you joking too?

LITTLE B: If I say 'yes,' will I get the job?

CALEB: I still need to see your resume.

LITTLE B: I need a resume?

CALEB: Usually that's what people do.

LITTLE B: I don't have one.

CALEB: You wanna be a clown?

LITTLE B: The ad said I could be other people too.

CALEB: Sure, you can be Cinderella, Ariel, Snow White, Pocahontas.
Just about any of the female characters.

LITTLE B: But I can't be myself.

CALEB: You can be yourself in a clown suit.

LITTLE B: Okay, then. I'll take the job.

CALEB: It's not exactly yours to take. You still have to interview.

LITTLE B: Isn't that what we're doing?

CALEB: I guess.

LITTLE B: Are you the manager?

CALEB: Yes.

LITTLE B: The one who hires people?

CALEB: Yes.

LITTLE B: And is there a job?

CALEB: Yes.

LITTLE B: Then can I have it?

CALEB: Sure.

LITTLE B: Really?

CALEB: You want it that bad, it's yours.

LITTLE B: Thank you very very much!

Elliot has been trying to contain himself.

ELLIOT: Can I speak yet?

LITTLE B: I got the job!

Elliot shakes Caleb's hand.

ELLIOT: She'll be your best clown, or Snow White, or whatever you want her to be.

CALEB: Good.

ELLIOT: She'll be great. Like, really, really great. I promise.

CALEB: You promise?

ELLIOT: Really, really great. I swear. She won't disappoint you. She's extremely dependable, reliable. You know, she's everything you'd want. In an employee. Or a clown. Or Snow White, or whatever. Like, she has a great imagination and she's just a really great worker, you know, and she's great with kids. You're going to love her. I know it. So that's what I wanted to say and, um, so yeah, I—yes, thanks, that's the other thing, just, just—thank you.

CALEB: You're welcome.

LITTLE B (*a loud whisper*): Hey Bobo?

CALEB (*mimicking her whisper*): What?

LITTLE B: My brother thinks you're cute.

ELLIOT (*embarrassed*): B—

CALEB: How do you know?

LITTLE B: He rambles around boys he likes.

Lights shift.

SCENE FIVE

Elliot, alone in his living room. He's gotten all gussied up for a date. He's sitting, looking at a bottle of wine and two empty glasses.

There's a knock at the door. Elliot answers it.

Caleb enters, still decked out in his clown get-up, and holding a duffel bag.

CALEB: Hi.
ELLIOT: Caleb, hi.
CALEB: I'm sorry I'm late.
ELLIOT: It's okay.

Elliot doesn't know how to react to the clown suit.

ELLIOT: I was gonna pour us some wine. Do you drink wine?
CALEB: Sure.

Elliot pours two glasses.

ELLIOT: It's red.

CALEB: I like red.

> *Elliot hands Caleb a glass, holds his up to toast.*

ELLIOT: Cheers.

> *They both drink.*

ELLIOT: I hope this isn't stating the obvious, but do you know that you're wearing a clown suit?

CALEB: Yeah.

ELLIOT: And makeup.

CALEB: I know.

ELLIOT: Just checking.

CALEB: I was late and I didn't want to be any later than I already was.

ELLIOT: Is this, like, your version of drag or something?

CALEB: No.

ELLIOT: Because if it is, I'm fine with that. I'd just like to know.

CALEB: No. I just...I got stuck at work.

ELLIOT: Okay.

CALEB: I literally made my last balloon animal fifteen minutes ago.

ELLIOT: It's okay.

> *Beat.*

Do you mind if we do something real quick?

CALEB: Do what?

ELLIOT: Play this game. It's not really a game, it's just something I like to do.

CALEB: Okay.

Elliot grabs a book off a shelf.

ELLIOT: Okay, so I'm thinking something in my head. It's a rule. Do you agree to abide by the rule that I have in my head?

CALEB: What is it?

ELLIOT: I can't tell you yet. You just have to trust me and agree.

CALEB: I agree.

ELLIOT: Now tell me when to stop.

Elliot begins flipping through pages.

CALEB: Stop.

Elliot stops. He holds the book open to the pages he's stopped on.

ELLIOT: Tell me when to stop.

Elliot alternates between the left page and the right page.

CALEB: Stop.

Elliot stops. He moves his finger up and down that page.

ELLIOT: One more time.

CALEB: Stop.

ELLIOT: Okay. So the rule that I had in my head was that whatever sentence I landed on would be our fortune. To give us an idea of what kind of future we might have.

CALEB: Shouldn't we get to know each other a little better before we find out what our future holds?

ELLIOT: You already agreed.

CALEB: Okay, then what's our fortune?

He reads whatever sentence his finger has landed on.

CALEB: So that's our future?

ELLIOT: I guess.

If it sounds good, they might smile at each other.

If it sounds bad, they might laugh it off, like, oh well.

41

If it doesn't make any sense, they might
laugh at that, and Elliot might say
something like: "Sometimes the book
doesn't know what it's talking about."

ELLIOT: You know, I've never seen you without it.

CALEB: Without what?

ELLIOT: The face paint, the suit, the...yeah. All of it.

CALEB: Oh, god—you totally distracted me. I was gonna change. And wash my face.

ELLIOT: That would be good. Don't get me wrong, you make an attractive clown—

CALEB: Thank you.

ELLIOT: —but it would be nice to see what you actually look like.

CALEB: This is kind of a weird thing to ask, but would you mind if I took a shower? I smell like birthday party.

ELLIOT: Sure. The bathroom's down the hall.

CALEB: Good. I brought my own towel and soap, and I've got date clothes in my duffel bag.

ELLIOT: You came prepared.

CALEB: The clown's life is nomadic. You have to be ready for anything. Oh my god I am such a dork.

ELLIOT: Wait, could you just, um...

CALEB: Yeah?

ELLIOT: Wait right here? For one minute.

CALEB: Okay.

ELLIOT: I'll be right back.

> *Elliot goes off. Caleb looks around Elliot's place.*
>
> *After a moment, Elliot returns with some wet towels and a bowl of water.*

ELLIOT: I'm impatient. You can use the shower, but...

> *Elliot removes Caleb's red clown hair.*

ELLIOT: I need...

> *He puts the wet towel up to Caleb's face.*

ELLIOT: To see your face first.

> *He slowly wipes Caleb's face clean of the clown makeup.*
>
> *When Caleb's face is totally bare, Elliot looks at it, takes him in.*

CALEB: Can I kiss you?

ELLIOT: Yes.

They kiss.

Lights stay on Elliot and Caleb, as they continue to kiss, slowly, tenderly.

SCENE SIX

Lights up on Kenny.

He talks to the audience, but is aware of the two men kissing.

KENNY: When I was growing up,
    my neighborhood was the perfect place.
    All of these families who knew each other
    and really loved each other.
    And there was a kid my age in almost every house on the block.
    And we all hung out at each other's houses after school.
    And then on holidays everyone would get together like we were
    all part of each other's families…
    Like, on Christmas, we'd all go down the street to the Stevenson
    house, and on Easter:
    we'd go to the Parker place, and on Memorial Day:
    everyone would come over to my house,
    and my dad would cook up hamburgers
    in the back
    on the barbecue.
    And my mom would end up drunk
    at the piano
    singing "The Way We Were."

A lot of my memories end with my mom drunk
at the piano
singing "The Way We Were."

> *Beat. Caleb and Elliot stop kissing.*
> *Caleb exits.*

> *Elsewhere, Barry enters. Elliot crosses to*
> *him, hands him some cash. They both*
> *begin undressing.*

But what I'm trying to get at is
how great this neighborhood used to be.
Here's the thing, though.
I'm still living in the same house, right?
I inherited it from my parents.
So my house is the same,
but pretty much everything else about the neighborhood has
changed.
The families have moved away
and there's been this influx of, um…these people.
You know, I'm not homophobic,
I just don't want to see it, you know? In front of my face.
Because seeing two guys kiss,
it just kind of makes me want to throw up.

Beat.

But these people,

I don't think they mean to ruin the neighborhood,

they're just generally ignorant.

I don't think they know what they've done to devalue my home.

And I'm not talking financially,

no—

I'm talking about how they've devalued my home

spiritually.

They've taken over—

and I don't use that phrase lightly,

I use it because it's true—they've taken over

and their takeover has been hostile.

And they make me sick, right?

For example:

The guys who live in the Stevenson house—

they're raising a kid,

which just seems wrong to me on so many levels.

Because that kid is gonna grow up with this warped perception of

the world and by the time he realizes that his so-called "parents"

are degenerates,

he'll probably be one too.

And that makes me feel sorry for him and I wish I didn't have to

see it happen.

And those guys who moved into the Parker place,

they're the kind that really flaunt it, right?

The kind who really shove it in your face.

And when I think about all the time that I used to hang out over there,

you know,

like all the times I went swimming with Danny Parker in their backyard,

or later, all the times Amy Parker and I fucked in her bedroom,

trying not to make too much noise so her parents wouldn't hear.

She was my first, you know?

So there's an extra bit of nostalgia connected to the place for me.

And then I think about the stuff that must go on in that house now,

and it makes me sick, right?

It makes me want to reclaim this neighborhood house by house.

It makes me want to show them that we won't just stand by silently

and watch them ruin everything that we built.

It makes me want to—

It makes me—

It makes me want to do something.

Lights shift.

SCENE SEVEN

Elliot lies in bed. Barry stands over him. They're both in various stages of undress. Role-playing:

ELLIOT: Dad, what are you doing here?

BARRY: I thought I'd check on you.

ELLIOT: But why aren't you with mom?

BARRY: Your mother has a headache.

ELLIOT: She kicked you out of bed?

BARRY: Yes.

ELLIOT: I'm sorry.

BARRY (*cautious, as himself*): Can I ask you a question, Tom?

ELLIOT: Yes, sir.

BARRY: No, stop. You like me, right?

ELLIOT: Yeah...

BARRY: I can't do this. I like you too. I don't mean to be judgmental, but—

ELLIOT: What do you mean?

BARRY: Okay. The father thing. Why do you like this?

Beat.

ELLIOT: What?

49

BARRY: It's just that, I've been with a lot of guys who had a lot of weird fetishes—some strange shit, you know? But for the most part, I think it's all pretty healthy. And then I've been with a few guys like you, who want the father thing. Which—I have to be honest—I think is twisted. Now, I wouldn't say anything about it to most guys because I don't like most of the guys who pay me to fuck them. So who cares, right? About them—who cares. But you're different. I like you. You're a nice guy. So tell me: why do you like this? Why do you need this?

ELLIOT: I don't know what to tell you.

BARRY: I don't mean to make you uncomfortable.

ELLIOT: I'm not—

BARRY: I was just—

ELLIOT: —uncomfortable.

BARRY: —curious.

Beat.

ELLIOT: Do you have any weird things that you like?

BARRY: No. It all feels good.

ELLIOT: But anything specific that you do when you're with a guy who doesn't pay you—

BARRY: I don't do that.

ELLIOT: What do you mean?

BARRY: Get with guys who don't pay me. I'm straight.

ELLIOT: Really?

BARRY: Yeah.

ELLIOT: But you fuck guys.

BARRY: For money. Why not? I'm good at fucking, I can fuck all
day—so why not get paid for it. I'd rather spend the day fucking
than sit behind a desk. And I can make triple the money with
guys. Something about my look. You like my look?

ELLIOT: Yeah.

BARRY: See. And I'm not a homophobe, so why not make the most of
what God gave me, right?

ELLIOT: I guess.

Beat.

ELLIOT: That's funny.

BARRY: What is?

ELLIOT: When you wanted to ask me a question, that's not what I
thought you were going to ask.

BARRY: What were you expecting?

ELLIOT (*changing the subject*): Isn't it weird about the building thing?

BARRY: What building thing?

ELLIOT: I live down the hall.

BARRY: You do?

ELLIOT: You didn't know?

BARRY: You live down the hall?

ELLIOT: Yeah. I almost didn't come over the first time because I
thought it might be awkward. Then when you opened your door, I

recognized you. But I wasn't sure if you recognized me because you didn't say anything, so I didn't say anything. You've never seen me?

BARRY: Are you over by the laundry room, in 2B?

ELLIOT: Yeah.

BARRY: You live with that girl, your...who is she?

ELLIOT: My sister.

BARRY: Yeah, okay, yeah. I've seen you two in the elevator. Your sister likes to wear her hair funny and sing. What's that about?

ELLIOT: It's what she does.

Beat.

BARRY: Are you going to the barbecue?

ELLIOT: I don't know. Look, could we just...

BARRY: What?

ELLIOT: Stop talking? I'm sorry. It's just that, I've done the whole try-to-be-friends-with-your-hustler thing, and I don't think it works, so I don't do it anymore. I've kind of made it a policy.

BARRY: A policy?

ELLIOT: I know that sounds weird, but—

BARRY: You'd rather just fuck?

ELLIOT: Yeah.

BARRY: Okay, but—

ELLIOT: But what?

BARRY: I'm not gonna be your dad.

ELLIOT: You're not?

BARRY: No. That's fucked. You need to grow up.

ELLIOT: I do?

BARRY: Yeah.

Awkward beat.

BARRY: So you were afraid this was gonna be awkward?

ELLIOT: Well—the building thing—

BARRY: Okay. Then you tell me—is this awkward?

> *Barry leans in, kisses Elliot, then pulls
> away and looks to Elliot for a response.*

ELLIOT: No.

BARRY: How about this. Is this awkward?

> *Barry puts his hand down the front of
> Elliot's pants, grabbing his cock.*

ELLIOT: No.

BARRY: And this...?

> *Barry leans in for another kiss, and then
> they give in to each other. Lights shift.*

SCENE EIGHT

*Caleb and his mom, Ruth, sit at The
French Market, a restaurant on Santa
Monica Blvd. They look at their menus.*

CALEB: So, how are things?

RUTH: They're fine.

CALEB: But how's dad?

RUTH: Oh, you know—

CALEB: Not really.

RUTH (*looking at the menu*): They have goulash. You love goulash.

CALEB: How's dad?

RUTH: The drugs seem to be helping.

CALEB: Yeah?

RUTH: His state of mind. It doesn't look like they'll do chemo.

CALEB: That's good, right?

RUTH: They don't think it'll help. More pain than it's worth.

Beat, as that sinks in.

CALEB: And you...?

RUTH: What about me?

CALEB: How are you?

RUTH: My knee's acting up again. And I think I might be going deaf.
   You could get a hamburger and fries. Not much they can do

wrong to a hamburger and fries.

CALEB: What do you mean you think you're going deaf?

RUTH: Unless there's Mad Cow again.

CALEB: Mom?

RUTH: It's probably wax, but we'll see. I have an appointment with
Dr. Stearn. What about fettuccini Alfredo? Do you like Alfredo?
Or do you still have lactose problems?

CALEB: Mom.

RUTH: What?

CALEB: I can read the menu.

RUTH: I know you can.

CALEB: You don't need to—

He stops himself.

RUTH: What?

CALEB: No, never mind.

RUTH: What?

CALEB: I'm thirty-three-years-old and I don't need you to—

RUTH: I'm sorry.

CALEB: —read the menu for me.

RUTH: It's a hard habit—

CALEB: I know.

RUTH: —to break.

CALEB: I know. But just worry about yourself, okay?

Beat.

RUTH: But what are you having?

CALEB: I don't know, I haven't decided.

Beat, as they continue to look at their menus.

RUTH: So, are you dating anyone?

CALEB: What?

RUTH: Are you dating anyone?

Caleb considers whether or not he should tell her about Elliot.

CALEB: Not really.

RUTH: What's "not really"?

CALEB: I don't know.

RUTH: How can you not know?

CALEB: I don't know if I am.

RUTH: How is that possible?

Caleb shakes his head, he doesn't have an answer.

RUTH: Did you call Kathryn Hoover?

CALEB: Mom.

RUTH: Did you?

CALEB: No.

RUTH: I gave you her number a month ago.

CALEB: I'm sorry.

RUTH: It makes me look bad.

CALEB: I'll call her.

RUTH: You say that—

CALEB: I will.

RUTH: —but then you don't.

CALEB: Mom.

RUTH: If you say you're going to do something, just do it.

CALEB: I told you I—

RUTH: I mean, how many times do I have to—

CALEB: Stop it.

RUTH: —ask you before you'll finally—

CALEB: Please stop.

RUTH: —do it? How many?

CALEB: I'm gonna go.

RUTH: No, stay.

CALEB: No, it's okay, you don't listen to me so I'm just gonna leave.

RUTH: Why, why?

CALEB: I sleep with men, mom. I've told you, like, a dozen fucking times. How many more times do I have to say it before you stop trying to fix me up with your friends' daughters?

RUTH: Calling Kathryn Hoover wouldn't kill you.

57

Beat.

CALEB: Bye.

He starts to go.

RUTH: Caleb? Please. Don't.

CALEB: What?

RUTH: Why do we have to do this all the time? I just don't understand why we have to talk about it all the time.

She looks to Caleb for an answer, but he still doesn't say anything.

RUTH: Why? Why? Because I heard you. The first time you told me, I heard you.

CALEB: You did?

RUTH: Yes, and I wish. You would stop. Talking about it. Why do gay people have to talk about it all the time?

CALEB: Why does it bother you so much?

RUTH: Because it bothers me.

Beat.

Because I've read up.

Believe me, I've done my research.

I've read the books.

I've read the magazines.

I've rented the films.

I've watched the news programs.

I've even searched the web.

I've culled my data.

You know, the thing that's...difficult...about being a parent,

is that you never know what your kid knows,

what your kid's not telling you,

what your kid's doing when you're not there.

So you have to fill in the blanks,

connect the dots.

And while I might not know what you,

my son,

specifically have done,

I do know what people say—

about you,

about you people,

your people,

about you and your people.

I know what you do, as a group.

I know about, about, about—

I know all about the anonymous sex.

I know about

sex with strangers,

in clubs—sex clubs—with towels around your waists.

About sex in places like public parks behind trees,

or urinals, public restrooms like George Michael,

or alleys, dark alleys, orgies in alleys,

multiple partners in one night, countless strangers.

I know about glory holes,

which I have to admit have a kind of spectacular name:

Glory Hole.

It paints a vivid picture:

Glory Hole.

I found this website that lists all of the glory holes in the world,

at least that's what the website purports,

and I'm inclined to believe it

because there are just so many bathrooms listed, it's...

dizzying.

And the website has all of this...data, I guess you'd call it. About

where to find the best glory holes in your area, and what time to

go, you know...when each hole hits heavy traffic. If you wanted

to get your penis sucked by a stranger during your lunch hour,

believe me, I could point you in the right direction.

I know about,

about,

about—

I know about leather bars, about bear bars.

About size queens, muscle queens, queen queens.

About Cock rings.

Anal Beads.

Lube.

Poppers.

I know there are other drugs, but poppers are so scary because
they could damage your brain, just like that, so you have to be
real careful.

And overdosing on Viagra, and things like that.

Because, you know,

the gay population is using a lot of Viagra these days.

And I know about, um,

um,

tops and bottoms, also known as "pitchers" and "catchers,"

and then there are versatile guys but I haven't read of a baseball
term that describes them.

I was thinking "he plays for both teams" might work

but then I found out that already means something else entirely.

And I know about, um,

two-headed dildos,

and things like that.

I don't really want to get into all of the sex toys

because they're kind of disgusting to me—

I can't even figure out what some of them are even used for,

I just know that they're disgusting.

Beat.

But what I'm trying to say is that there are all of

these,

these,

these images in my head.

And you have to understand that these

images

sometimes make you a very difficult person to talk to.

But that's not all.

Because I know it's not just difficult for me.

I'm not that self-absorbed.

I'm not that—

I know how you...

I know, I know—

I mean, I don't *know*, but I can imagine,

how difficult it must have been for you,

must *be* for you,

to—

oh, God, to, to—

To come out.

To have that conversation.

To keep having that conversation.

To keep having to have that—

It must have been so hard.

When you said it the first time.

The fear of rejection.

The fear of other things.

The fear of—

I tried not to reject you when you told me.

Because I suspected.

Your son reaches his twenties without ever bringing a girl home

and you start to suspect.

And I saw the way you looked at your, you know,

male friends

and the way you weren't looking at your, you know,

female friends.

So I prepared myself,

just in case,

so as not to have the reaction I didn't want to have, which was

one of rejecting you.

But, Caleb, honey...

You have to understand

that if *I'm* having these thoughts—

I, your mother—

if these thoughts are in my head,

then just think about what other people must be thinking.

I can't help it.

And what I've read,

what I've seen—

which hasn't all been bad.

I don't want to give you that impression...

Beat.

But people are backwards,

people don't understand,

people have a long way to go, you know?

And when they see you,

what some of them are thinking,

what I know some of them are thinking—

I mean, when they see you, I know they're not: Seeing. You.

They're seeing—

They're—

Beat. She's begun to run out of steam.

And I know about Matt Shepard.

Everyone calls him Matthew, but I read somewhere that his friends called him Matt.

I know what happened to him.

And my first thought is that plenty of straight people die worse deaths than he did without getting put on a pedestal. Without getting idealized. Without becoming heroes.

But I understand why he haunts us.

Because it's just terrible what they did to him.

And you could say it was just a moment of passion,

but that defense doesn't stick because they just spent too much time with him.

They lured him into their truck.

And then they started beating him.

And then they continued to beat him as they drove him out to the fence.

The fence where they were going to leave him.

I know all about Matt Shepard.

And things like what happened to him—they could happen to the rest of us too,

but when you factor in a thing like sexuality,

the chances of something like that happening to my son,

they triple, or something terrible like that.

And that scares me, Caleb. It really, really scares me.

Beat.

And I know about AIDS.

And I know you don't want me to say it,

but I'm a mother,

so I'm going to say it:

You need to wear a condom,

and your partner needs to wear a condom—

because things were better for awhile,

but lately people have become lackadaisical,

and the figures are rising.

So just wear a condom.

Just do it.

For me.

Because the thought of you getting AIDS

scares the shit out of me.

I'm sorry.

I'm sorry that I'm like this.

I don't mean to sound like a Public Service Announcement.

But I'm a mother,

I'm your mother,

and I just—

I don't want you to get hurt.

That's all.

Beat.

That's all.

So.

What are you having for lunch?

CALEB: The fettuccini.

Lights shift.

SCENE NINE

Elliot, alone in his living room, grading papers.

There's a knock at the door. Elliot opens it, finds Caleb.

CALEB: What are you doing?

ELLIOT: Grading papers.

CALEB: Do you have a second?

ELLIOT: Yeah.

CALEB: Can I kiss you?

ELLIOT: You don't always have to—

They kiss.

ELLIOT: —ask.

They both enter the apartment.

CALEB: I need to ask you something else. I just, I—. Okay, I'll just say it: Do you want to be my boyfriend?

Beat.

ELLIOT: What?

CALEB: Will you be?

ELLIOT: You want me to be your boyfriend?

CALEB: That's what I just said. Will you?

ELLIOT: I've never been a boyfriend.

CALEB: I know.

ELLIOT: I've never really thought of myself as boyfriend material. I can't believe you want to be my—. I mean, I've had relationships. I have, just never to the point where we called each other boyfriend or anything...You know, actually, I guess I haven't had that many relationships, really. They don't count if they only lasted one night and I had to pay for them, do they? I'm joking. Kind of. Okay, now I'm rambling. I'm sorry. I should stop talking, but I just. Okay, wow, geez. I guess I'm kind of nervous right now because the idea gets me really excited. The idea of having a boyfriend. Of being a boyfriend. The idea of...yeah. I mean, yeah. Yeah, yeah, yeah. The idea of having someone I could actually...yes. It sounds good. It sounds...like something I've never had...before. Yes, yes, a boyfriend, yes, that's something I'd definitely like.

CALEB: You're sure?

ELLIOT: I've never been so sure of anything in my entire life.

Beat.

CALEB: So I'm your first boyfriend?

68

ELLIOT: In thirty years. I'm assuming you've had several boyfriends.

Beat.

Have you had several boyfriends? We should probably have that conversation. Now that we're boyfriends.

CALEB: A couple. The last one, we were together a long time.

ELLIOT: How long's a long time?

CALEB: Two years.

ELLIOT: Why'd you—

CALEB: Split up?

ELLIOT: Yeah.

CALEB: Okay, here we go: He realized he was a furry.

ELLIOT: What do you mean?

CALEB: He was a furry.

ELLIOT: Like he just realized one day that he had a lot of hair?

CALEB: You've never heard of furries?

ELLIOT: No.

CALEB: They're like people who are into Ren Faire, but instead of dressing up like medieval times, they dress up like rabbits and bears and, you know, furry animals.

ELLIOT: You're joking, right?

CALEB: Swear to God.

ELLIOT: What was he? A little bunny rabbit?

CALEB: No.

ELLIOT: A grizzly bear?

CALEB: No, I'm not gonna—

ELLIOT: Was he a possum?

CALEB: He was a fox.

Beat.

ELLIOT: You're totally pulling my leg.

CALEB: I swear. He had a whole outfit, you know. A whole furry fox outfit.

ELLIOT: That is so...wait.

CALEB: What?

ELLIOT: Is this you asking me in a kind of roundabout way if I'll wear a furry fox outfit the next time we do it?

CALEB: No.

ELLIOT: Because I could probably find a fuzzy little tail.

CALEB: I'd rather you didn't.

ELLIOT: Don't be shy.

CALEB: I don't know why I told you about the furry thing.

ELLIOT: You told me because we're boyfriends and boyfriends tell each other everything.

CALEB: Yeah, I guess you're right.

ELLIOT: So tell me the truth—is this Furry thing a fetish of yours?

CALEB: You aren't gonna let me live this down, are you?

ELLIOT: No, it's not that. I just want to know because if that's what you like, I'll do it. I'll do whatever you want. After all, you are my boyfriend.

CALEB: I promise you, it was his thing, not mine.

ELLIOT: I just like using the word boyfriend. In sentences that refer to me and someone else. You should take advantage of that, if you know what's good for you. Like, if you have any really weird fetishes, like weirder than the fur thing, I would put 'em on the table now while I'm still too fixated on the word 'boyfriend' to find anything else strange.

CALEB: I'll keep that in mind, boyfriend.

ELLIOT: Okay, now it doesn't even sound like a word anymore.

Beat.

CALEB: How about you?

ELLIOT: What?

CALEB: You have any weird fetishes I should know about?

ELLIOT: I kind of set myself up for that, didn't I?

CALEB: You're avoiding the question.

Beat.

ELLIOT: I've got one. But I'm working on it.

Lights shift.

SCENE TEN

The apartment BBQ. Elliot and Kenny
are standing, awkward.

KENNY: I've been neglecting my girlfriend.
ELLIOT: I'm sorry. I—
KENNY: So I'll be going.
ELLIOT: It was nice to meet you.

Kenny exits. Elliot looks at his chicken:
he doesn't feel like eating it anymore.

Another man, Barry, approaches the
table for some food. He glances at Elliot,
then gives a smile of recognition.

BARRY: Hi.

Elliot looks embarrassed. He smiles
back, weakly.

BARRY: How are you?
ELLIOT: I'm fine. I'm okay. You?
BARRY: I'm good.
ELLIOT: Why do people ask that?

BARRY: "How are you?"

ELLIOT: Yeah. I mean, do you really care?

BARRY: Yes.

ELLIOT: I'm sorry, I'm being...Can we start over?

BARRY: Okay.

ELLIOT: And could we forget that we ever, you know...

BARRY: Why?

ELLIOT: I'm trying to phase a few things out of my life.

BARRY: Like sex?

ELLIOT: Like transactions—

BARRY: That result in sex.

ELLIOT: Yeah, that's what I'm—

BARRY: That's what you're trying to phase out. Sure. Whatever you want.

ELLIOT: Really?

BARRY: Sure. So, hi. I'm Barry.

ELLIOT: I'm Elliot.

BARRY: I thought your name was Tom.

ELLIOT: I thought we were forgetting last week.

BARRY: We were. I just wanted to clarify.

ELLIOT: I lied to you. It's really Elliot.

BARRY: Okay...So, Elliot, what do you do for fun?

ELLIOT: I don't really have that much fun. I teach high school. I grade papers. I take care of my sister, she's fifteen. But I just started seeing someone and he's fun, so I guess I'm having more fun lately than usual. I don't want to jinx it, but it's, you know—

73

BARRY: It's going good.

ELLIOT: Yeah. I think it's the real deal.

BARRY: You play golf?

ELLIOT: Only mini.

BARRY: I can play mini. You think you and this guy might want to go to Golf 'N' Stuff with me sometime?

ELLIOT: So, like, a friend thing?

BARRY: Yeah, I know you have that policy about not socializing with—

ELLIOT: But that never happened. So let's do it. Let's be friends.

BARRY: You sure?

ELLIOT: Yeah. That'd be good. I don't really have any straight friends.

BARRY: Why not?

ELLIOT: I don't know why I said that. I don't really have any gay friends either. I don't really have many friends in general. I'd like a "circle of friends." I don't have a "circle." Do you have a "circle"?

BARRY: Not quite a circle, more like a line. I'd like a circle, though.

ELLIOT: Yeah, me too.

Lights shift.

SCENE ELEVEN

Mom and Elliot sit together at The French Market, looking at menus.

ELLIOT: So, how are things?

MOM: I need to tell you something.

ELLIOT: Me too.

MOM: You go first. No, wait, first let's decide what we're having for lunch. What are you having for lunch?

ELLIOT: The fettuccine Alfredo. And I'm in love.

MOM: What?

ELLIOT: Okay, I went first. I'm in love. That's what I needed to tell you.

MOM: Is he in love with you?

ELLIOT: Yeah, mom.

MOM: Oh, honey, I'm so happy. That's wonderful news.

ELLIOT: His name is Caleb.

MOM: I almost named you Caleb.

ELLIOT: I know.

MOM: It was between Elliot and Caleb.

ELLIOT: I know.

MOM: My son's in love with a man named Caleb. Who would've thought, when I had you thirty years ago, that we'd be having this conversation one day?

ELLIOT: He's a really good guy. Like, unbelievably good.

MOM: Good.

ELLIOT: He's the only guy I've ever known who I feel like I can be still with. Does that make sense?

MOM: Yes.

ELLIOT: Okay, so now you can decide what you're having for lunch. And then you can tell me what you wanted to tell me. I just needed to get my news out, like, immediately. Do I seem different to you? I feel different.

MOM: Different how?

ELLIOT: I feel like a 16-year-old girl. Seriously. But do I look different? I mean, can you tell?

MOM: I can tell.

ELLIOT: But do I glow or anything?

MOM: You glow a little bit. I've never seen you smile so much.

ELLIOT: Really?

MOM: Yeah. But I should make a confession. I already knew about Caleb. Little B told me about him.

ELLIOT: What did she say?

MOM: She said that when she sees you two together, it makes her want to wear nail polish. And she told me that he's a clown. That's all I know about him. Tell me something else. What's he like?

ELLIOT: Well, he's kind of weird, like I am, but maybe weirder, which I think is why I was attracted to him in the first place. And he's sweet, and good, and considerate, and passionate, and funny. And he's great with Little B. You should see them together. She really loves her job. And it makes me feel like she's going to be okay, you know? Who knew it would take her getting a job as a clown to make me see that? It's such an odd profession. You know, Caleb was gonna be a lawyer. When he was a kid, it was a toss up between clown and lawyer. If that isn't weird, I don't know what is.

MOM: So you're telling me you could be dating a lawyer right now?

ELLIOT: But if he was a lawyer, he never would've started up Clown Town. And then he never would have given Little B a job. And then we never would've met. Maybe everything happens for a reason. I don't know. All I know is that I'm in love, Mom. And so is he, apparently, which is the main reason why he's weird—he likes me.

MOM: I want to meet him. Can I meet him?

ELLIOT: Of course.

MOM: Good.

ELLIOT: Now what did you want to tell me?

MOM: I'm in love too, his name is Avi, and he's twenty-five-years old.

Lights shift.

77

SCENE TWELVE

*Rose's baby shower. Becky, Kristen,
Little B, and Mom sit around Rose as she
opens presents.*

KRISTEN: You have an eyelash on your cheek.

*She scoops it up with her finger and then
presents it to Rose.*

BECKY: Make a wish...

LITTLE B: Wish for something amazing.

ROSE: Okay.

*She closes her eyes, makes a wish, and
blows.*

MOM: What did you wish for?

ROSE: I can't tell you.

MOM: Why not?

LITTLE B: Mom. Because it won't come true if she says it.

KRISTEN: Everyone knows that.

MOM: Well, I'm sorry.

Elliot enters.

ELLIOT: Rose...

ROSE: There you are.

MOM: We're already opening presents.

BECKY: You said not to wait.

ELLIOT: I know, I know.

MOM: Sit down.

ELLIOT: I will, but Rose—

ROSE: What?

ELLIOT: I have a surprise. Not for you, exactly; just something
　　　everyone's been asking me about. Well, someone.

MOM: He's here?

BECKY: Wait, the guy? You brought the guy?

KRISTEN: The one you've been seeing?

ROSE: Where is he?

LITTLE B (*singing "It's Oh So Quiet" from* Post; *a rush of energy*):
　　　"You fall in love! Zing, boom! The sky up above—zing,
　　　boom!—is caving in…WOW! FUN!"

ELLIOT: Okay, calm down, everyone. He's on the porch. I wanted to
　　　come in first and let you know he was here, so you don't all
　　　pounce on him the second he walks in.

KRISTEN: We won't pounce.

ROSE: We promise.

BECKY: I might pounce just a little bit.

KRISTEN: I'll hold her back, don't worry—no pouncing.

ELLIOT: This is so surreal. I can't believe I'm actually bringing a guy
　　　home.

MOM: Well, stop talking about it and let him in. We wanna meet him!

Lights shift.

SCENE THIRTEEN

Caleb stands on the porch, Elliot enters from the house.

ELLIOT: Alright, they're ready for you.

CALEB: I'm nervous.

ELLIOT: Don't be. They love you already. They haven't even met you, and they love you.

CALEB: You're sure?

ELLIOT: They're gonna treat you like the fucking Messiah, believe me.

CALEB: Okay, then let me go over this one more time. Your mom is Rose. Your older sister is Becky; her girlfriend is Kristen; their daughter is also Rose.

ELLIOT: Named after my mom.

CALEB: Right. And it's her baby shower.

ELLIOT: And don't forget Little B.

CALEB: I know B, I'm not worried about B.

ELLIOT: You've got it, you're golden.

CALEB: One last thing. I need you to kiss me for good luck.

They kiss. Damien approaches. Caleb and Elliot stop kissing. They look at the young man.

DAMIEN: Who the fuck are you?

ELLIOT: Who the fuck are you?

DAMIEN: Damien.

ELLIOT: The Damien?

DAMIEN: I guess.

ELLIOT: Damien Demeter?

DAMIEN: What do you care?

ELLIOT: I'm just glad to meet you. You're here to see Rose?

DAMIEN: No.

ELLIOT: You're not here to see Rose?

DAMIEN: Well I was, but I'm not.

ELLIOT: You're just gonna go?

Damien doesn't say anything.

ELLIOT: She wants to see you.

DAMIEN: You never answered my question.

ELLIOT: Who the fuck am I?

DAMIEN: Yeah.

ELLIOT: I'm her Uncle Elliot.

DAMIEN: Who's he?

ELLIOT: This is Caleb.

CALEB: I'm Elliot's boyfriend.

Damien looks at Caleb: gross.

ELLIOT: Why are you leaving?

DAMIEN: Don't tell her I was here, okay?

ELLIOT: No, wait—

> *Damien exits.*

Damien, wait!

> *Lights shift.*

SCENE FOURTEEN

Elliot re-enters the baby shower, with Caleb.

ELLIOT: Everyone, this is Caleb. Caleb, this is...everyone.

CALEB: Hi.

LITTLE B: Hello, Bobo.

CALEB: Hi, B. Alright, let me guess. (to Rose) Rose, right?

ROSE: How'd you know?

CALEB (*to Mom*): Becky?

MOM: You're too sweet. Call me Mom.

CALEB: Hi Mom.

(*to Becky*)

So you're Becky.

BECKY: Nice to meet you Caleb.

CALEB: (*to Kristen*) And you must be Kristen.

KRISTEN: Guilty as charged.

LITTLE B: Bobo, we were in the middle of opening presents...

CALEB: Oh, then continue, please...

BECKY: Okay, now that everyone's here, we can give you your big present.

MOM: This is mostly from your mother and Kristen.

BECKY: But everybody contributed.

Becky hands Rose an envelope. She opens it.

ROSE (*disbelief*): You're kidding me.

BECKY: No, that's real.

ROSE: What is this?

BECKY: A lot of stripping.

ROSE: But this is so much money.

KRISTEN: It's our tips from the last five months.

BECKY: Most of them.

LITTLE B: And my tips from my first two birthday parties.

BECKY: And your Grandma and Elliot put in some money too.

ELLIOT: A little bit.

CALEB: I contributed nothing.

ROSE: But this is crazy. This is way too much money.

BECKY: You need something—a nest egg—to help get you started.

ROSE: You're not kicking me out, are you?

BECKY: No. We're just...helping you assume responsibility.

KRISTEN: It's money we'd spend on the baby anyway. We want you to manage it.

ROSE: How do you know I won't blow it?

BECKY: Because I have faith in you. Because I can tell you're gonna be a better mom than that.

KRISTEN: And because she'd kill you.

BECKY: That too.

ROSE: This is crazy.

ELLIOT: You deserve it, kid.

ROSE: Thank you. Thank you all so much. This is the most amazing shower. I can't even believe it. It just freaks me out to think about how good everything is; that my kid's gonna grow up with all of this. It's almost perfect. Thank you.

Lights shift.

SCENE FIFTEEN

Rose's living room. Elliot and Rose do Lamaze breathing exercises.

ELLIOT: So as your labor progresses, your contractions are going to get worse and more frequent.

ROSE: Okay.

ELLIOT: And you want to match them in intensity with your breathing.

ROSE: All right.

ELLIOT: Start slowly and let it build every 10 seconds. On your mark, get set, go.

> *Rose breathes in and out through her mouth. Slowly at first, as Elliot counts off from his watch.*

ELLIOT: ...ten...

> *Rose picks up the pace slightly.*

ELLIOT: ...twenty...

> *Rose collapses into her belly and sighs.*

ELLIOT: Okay, stop, what are you doing?

ROSE: I feel like I'm gonna hyperventilate.

ELLIOT: I can fix that.

ROSE: How?

ELLIOT: You're supposed to breathe in the tempo of a song.

ROSE: Why?

ELLIOT: To forget that you're breathing.

ROSE: I'm supposed to forget that I'm breathing so I don't forget to
    breathe?

ELLIOT: Exactly.

ROSE: What song?

ELLIOT: The book suggests "Yellow Submarine."

ROSE: No. Fucking. Way.

ELLIOT: Then pick something.

ROSE: Anything I want?

ELLIOT: Anything you want.

ROSE: Okay, done.

ELLIOT: Nine Inch Nails?

ROSE (*she nods*): "Head Like a Hole."

ELLIOT: Good choice.

ROSE: Thanks.

ELLIOT: Okay, start breathing.

> *Rose breathes the Nine Inch Nails song,*
> *while Elliot counts to himself.*

ELLIOT: ...ten...

Rose's breathing of the song intensifies.

ELLIOT: ...twenty...

Rose's breathing continues to intensify.

ELLIOT: ...twenty-five...

By now, Rose is practically head-banging.

ELLIOT: ...thirty. Stop. Good job!

ROSE: Really?

ELLIOT: Did you hyperventilate?

ROSE: Almost.

ELLIOT: Then we're almost there.

ROSE: This is retarded.

ELLIOT: You're retarded.

ROSE: Shut up, I'm serious. You shouldn't be doing this with me.

ELLIOT: Why not?

ROSE: Damien should be doing this.

ELLIOT: Well.

ROSE: I love you and all, but I just wish—

ELLIOT: I know.

ROSE: Wait.

ELLIOT: What?

ROSE: You understand guys, don't you?

ELLIOT: Sometimes.

ROSE: But you're a guy and you like guys, so you must have a better understanding of guys than the rest of us.

ELLIOT: Not really.

ROSE: Why doesn't Damien want anything to do with me?

ELLIOT: I don't know.

ROSE: I feel like such an asshole, you know? Like I should stop calling and sending him letters. Like I should just get the message. I mean, I'm practically stalking him. I don't know what else to do. I still want him in my life. You know?

ELLIOT: I know.

ROSE: Uncle Elliot?

ELLIOT: Yeah?

ROSE: Did you know my dad?

ELLIOT: Why?

ROSE: When my mom got pregnant with me...

ELLIOT: Yeah?

ROSE: And ran away from home...

ELLIOT: Yeah?

ROSE: What was so bad about my dad that made her want to have me without him?

Beat.

ROSE: What?

ELLIOT: A lot of things, Rose.

ROSE: But what?

Beat.

She won't talk about him. I feel like it's my right to know.

Beat.

You won't tell me?

ELLIOT: I've been meaning to give you something.

ROSE: What is it?

ELLIOT: Just something I want you to have.

Elliot hands her an old book with a broken spine.

ELLIOT: Look inside.

ROSE: This is your journal.

ELLIOT: From when I was fifteen, sixteen.

ROSE: Are you sure...?

ELLIOT: After your mom ran away. The summer Little B was born.

It'll answer some of your questions.

ROSE: Okay.

ELLIOT: There's some funny baby stuff too. I spent a lot of time with
Little B.

ROSE: What was she like before she was Bjork?

ELLIOT: A regular kid.

ROSE: Do you think she'll ever be normal again?

ELLIOT: I don't know. But I do know that if we don't get back to
these exercises, you're gonna forget how to breathe when you
give birth. So one, two, three: breathe in.

Lights shift.

SCENE SIXTEEN

We hear the sound of a school bell ringing. We're in the Chatsworth High band room.

Damien Demeter is alone, dismantling his clarinet, putting it away. Rose stands at the door, holding a sealed manila envelope.

ROSE: Hi.

DAMIEN: What are you doing here?

ROSE: You won't even say hello?

DAMIEN: Don't freak.

ROSE: I'm not.

DAMIEN: It's just that I thought you dropped out.

ROSE: I'm finishing my classes at home.

DAMIEN: So why are you here?

ROSE: I had to pick up my Algebra final from Mr. Spencer.

DAMIEN: The final isn't until next week.

ROSE: I know.

DAMIEN (*motioning to the envelope Rose is holding*): Is that it?

ROSE: Yeah.

DAMIEN: Can I borrow it?

ROSE: No.

DAMIEN: How does Mr. Spencer know you aren't gonna cheat?

ROSE: He trusts me.

DAMIEN: But you could.

ROSE: My mom's giving it to me. So, really, I can't. Look, this isn't—

DAMIEN: What?

ROSE: I need to talk to you, okay?

DAMIEN: I heard that your mom's a stripper.

ROSE: What?

DAMIEN: I heard she's a Lesbian, too.

ROSE: So?

DAMIEN: And that her girlfriend's, like, living with you.

ROSE: What the fuck do you care?

DAMIEN: I care, okay? It's just that you seem so different.

ROSE: Yeah, I'm pregnant.

DAMIEN: I've heard all of these...things...about you.

ROSE: Like what?

Damien doesn't respond.

What did you hear?

Again, no response.

Okay, listen, we need to talk. So, I came here to see you because part of me thought that maybe you and I could have another chance, that we never finished what we started. I mean, obviously

94

we haven't finished, because look at me, but the way you're acting right now, I feel like you hate me, like you'd be fine if you never talked to me again...Feel free to contradict me anytime.

Beat. No response from Damien.

Okay, so anyway. Here's the deal. I've spent most of my life alone. I grew up without a family—just my mom. And it was tough. And for a long time, things were really fucked up with us, but at least we had each other, so we weren't totally alone, right? And then six months ago, my mom randomly bumped into her brother Elliot, my uncle. And that, like, changed my whole life. Because, see, this is what happened. Before I was born, my mom ran away from home. So she always had a family, but they weren't a part of our lives. And now they are. So, whereas before I just had my mom, now I have an uncle. And an aunt. And a grandmother. And on top of all that, my mom's in love—which you can make fun of, but the fact is, I've never seen her so happy, and that's a good thing. And my baby is going to have two grandmothers instead of one, and that's a lucky baby in my book and fuck you for not recognizing that. Look, are you ever going to say anything?

Beat.

You're an asshole. I never saw that before—how much of an

asshole you really are. But even if you are an asshole, I have to think about what's best for this kid, you know? That I'm gonna have. And it seems to me that the best thing for my son would be for him to know his father. I never knew my father. I don't even know who he is. Can you imagine how hard that can be? I try to tell myself it's fine, you know? To trick myself into thinking it doesn't hurt. But the truth is, I would give anything to know where I came from. Even if my father was an asshole like you. Just knowing would make it better, I think.

Beat.

Are you ever gonna say anything? You're just gonna stand there?

Beat.

Fine. I thought you might want to know your son someday. I'm here to give you the option. You don't have to like me. You don't even have to be nice to me. Just don't disappear. For your son's sake, okay? I'm, like, having a shower tomorrow night, at my house. It's just family. But that includes you now, whether you like it or not, so you should come if you want to be part of this. If you want to be part of your son's life.

Beat.

DAMIEN: You...

ROSE: What?

DAMIEN: ...said...

ROSE: Yeah?

DAMIEN: ...son.

ROSE: Are you Tarzan?

DAMIEN: No.

ROSE: So can you say more than one syllable?

DAMIEN: Yeah...

Beat

You're having a boy?

ROSE: Yeah.

DAMIEN: What does it feel like?

ROSE: What do you mean?

DAMIEN: Being pregnant.

ROSE: It feels like you have to poop, but the poop wants to come out
of your pussy.

DAMIEN: That's disgusting.

ROSE: It was a dumb question.

*Damien approaches Rose, touches her
belly tenderly.*

DAMIEN: Being pregnant makes you look fat.

ROSE: You're not supposed to say things like that.

DAMIEN: But you look bigger than I thought you would.

ROSE: You thought about what I would look like?

DAMIEN: Of course.

> *They kiss. Suddenly, Rose breaks away*
> *from him.*

ROSE: What the fuck is going on right now?

DAMIEN: What do you mean?

ROSE: I mean, like, did you hear anything I just said to you?

DAMIEN: Yeah. I heard you.

ROSE: And what do you think about it?

DAMIEN: I can't really do this right now. I have to go, I'm late.

ROSE: Where do you have to go?

DAMIEN: I just have somewhere I have to go.

ROSE: But you never do anything.

DAMIEN: Look, I'm in the school play, okay? And rehearsals start in
    five minutes.

ROSE: They start in five minutes?

DAMIEN: Yeah.

ROSE: At three-twelve?

DAMIEN: Something like that.

ROSE: Okay, but—

DAMIEN: What?

ROSE: Really quick.

DAMIEN: Yeah?

ROSE: Did you get the poems I sent you?

DAMIEN: Yeah.

ROSE: And?

DAMIEN: Rose, look, I'm sorry, but I'm really late.

Beat. She just stares at him.

DAMIEN: I'll call you later or something.

Beat.

DAMIEN: Rose? Say something...Okay, well, I'll talk to you later.

She's still staring. He leaves the classroom.

ROSE: You forgot your clarinet.

Lights shift.

SCENE SEVENTEEN

Becky, Rose and Kristen's living room.

Little B is sitting, alone, practicing making balloon animals. There's a knock at the door.

LITTLE B: Coming!

She opens the door. It's Damien.

DAMIEN: Hi.

LITTLE B: Who are you?

DAMIEN: Who are you?

LITTLE B: That's what I just said.

DAMIEN: Well?

LITTLE B: I asked you first.

DAMIEN: I'm Damien.

LITTLE B: My name's Little B. Some people call me Bjork.

DAMIEN: Where's Rose?

LITTLE B: Do you know Rose?

DAMIEN: Yes.

LITTLE B: This is her house.

DAMIEN: What are you doing here?

LITTLE B: Getting ready for my job.

DAMIEN: What's your job?

LITTLE B: I make children happy.

DAMIEN: What are those balloons supposed to be?

LITTLE B: (*She can say whatever it is she's making.*)

DAMIEN: They don't look like (*whatever Little B said*).

LITTLE B: They're practice.

DAMIEN: So you don't know where Rose is, then?

LITTLE B: (*singing*) "Possibly maybe..."

DAMIEN: Is she here?

LITTLE B: Who are you?

DAMIEN: Damien.

LITTLE B: You said that already, but who are you?

DAMIEN: I'm a friend of Rose's.

LITTLE B: Wait a minute.

DAMIEN: What?

LITTLE B: Did you say your name was Damien?

DAMIEN: Yes.

LITTLE B: Damien Demeter?

DAMIEN: Yeah.

LITTLE B: Then I know who you are.

DAMIEN: Who am I?

LITTLE B: The father of her baby.

DAMIEN: Maybe.

LITTLE B: You had sex with her, right?

DAMIEN: Yeah.

LITTLE B: So that's who you are.

DAMIEN: How do I know she didn't have sex with a lot of other guys?

LITTLE B: Because she didn't.

DAMIEN: Monkey see, monkey do.

LITTLE B: What's that mean?

DAMIEN: You haven't told me who you are.

LITTLE B: I'm her aunt.

DAMIEN: The retarded one?

LITTLE B: I'm not retarded.

DAMIEN: How old are you, Bjork?

LITTLE B: You can call me Rebecca.

DAMIEN: How old are you, Rebecca?

LITTLE B: I'm fifteen.

DAMIEN: So is Rose.

LITTLE B: It's her birthday next week.

DAMIEN: Don't you think that's kind of weird? That your niece is older than you?

LITTLE B: No.

DAMIEN: You're going to hell, you know.

LITTLE B: What do you mean?

DAMIEN: Your whole family is like a factory for faggots.

Beat. Little B looks hurt.

So you don't know where Rose is?

LITTLE B: I told you I do.

DAMIEN: Where is she?

LITTLE B: She's at Lamaze.

DAMIEN: Who's she with?

LITTLE B: My brother.

DAMIEN: He's gay.

LITTLE B: I know.

DAMIEN: When does she come back?

LITTLE B: I don't know.

DAMIEN: I have to go to rehearsal.

LITTLE B: So?

DAMIEN: We're doing *A Midsummer Night's Dream*.

LITTLE B: I don't care.

DAMIEN: So I can't really wait for her.

Little B doesn't respond.

DAMIEN: Just give her these, okay?

He hands Little B several pieces of paper.

LITTLE B: What are they?

DAMIEN: Poems she wrote for me.

LITTLE B: What should I tell her?

DAMIEN: Tell her I want my clarinet back.

He starts to go, then stops. He looks back at Little B.

DAMIEN: And tell her I don't want to be part of his life.

Lights shift.

SCENE EIGHTEEN

The high school parking lot. It's 9 p.m.
Rose and Little B stand underneath a
street lamp. Rose holds a grocery bag.
Little B has Damien's clarinet.

ROSE: There's his car.

LITTLE B: He was really very weird. He didn't know who I was at
first.

ROSE: Did he say anything else?

Little B looks away from Rose at
Damien's car.

ROSE: After he gave you my stuff? After he gave up his parental
rights?

LITTLE B: No.

ROSE: I have to show him that he can't disrespect my son like that.

LITTLE B: He didn't believe I was your aunt.

ROSE: Do you want to throw the first one or should I?

LITTLE B: "When I was younger I used to play with the cat a lot—I
would teach it how to fly. Because, you see, he used to watch all
the birds flying about and I could tell he wanted to fly and chill
with the birds. I wasn't very successful though."

ROSE: Okay, I'll throw the first one.

LITTLE B: What if he comes out and sees us?

ROSE: He has rehearsal until ten. I checked...Hey, B, if you don't want to do this, you could just be my lookout.

LITTLE B: "I've been called weird since I was three or four. I had got used to it by the age of five. I made a decision then: I'd either live my life by what people thought of me and to a set of rules which I didn't really know or understand. Which would make me incredibly unhappy. Or I could just do what I wanted. And that's a lot more fun, isn't it? Call me a freak for thinking that, but it's what I do."

ROSE: So you're in?

LITTLE B: Yes.

Rose takes a carton of eggs out of the grocery bag. She opens it. Takes out an egg and throws it at Damien's car.

ROSE: Fucker!

Little B takes an egg and throws.

LITTLE B: Fucker!

Rose takes another egg and throws it. Then another, until she's thrown the entire carton.

ROSE: Asshole!...Bastard!...I hate you!...Fucker!

Rose's rage increases with each throw.

ROSE: Give me the clarinet.

Little B hands her Damien's instrument.

Rose smashes the clarinet against the street lamppost.

Suddenly, water pours down her legs.

LITTLE B: You're peeing.
ROSE: No, this is too soon.
LITTLE B: What's going on?
ROSE: I'm having the baby.

Lights shift.

SCENE NINETEEN

The sound of thump-thump-thumping electronica music.

We're on a street corner in West Hollywood, outside a dance club. The name of the dance club, "Heaven," hangs above the door in bright neon. Elliot and Caleb exit out of the club onto the street corner.

ELLIOT: I love you. I love you. I love you so much it kind of freaks me out.

They kiss.

ELLIOT: I need to tell you something.
CALEB: Wait.
ELLIOT: What?
CALEB: I forgot my jacket.
ELLIOT: No, wait, let me—
CALEB: Hold on. I'll be right back.

Elliot watches Caleb run back into the club. Elliot's cell phone rings.

ELLIOT: Hello? Hi Becky, what's—what do you mean? Okay, I'm coming. Don't freak out, she's gonna be alright. Okay, I'm on my way...It's gonna be okay, Becky. You're gonna be a Grandma. Don't freak out...I love you too.

Kenny approaches. Elliot doesn't recognize him.

KENNY: Hey, you.

ELLIOT: Yeah?

KENNY: Why are you smiling like that?

ELLIOT: My niece is about to have a baby.

KENNY: So what are you up to?

ELLIOT: What do you mean?

KENNY: Why are you smiling like that?

ELLIOT: I told you, I—

Elliot tries to walk by Kenny. Kenny blocks his way.

ELLIOT: Excuse me.

KENNY: Do you wanna be gay with me?

ELLIOT: What?

KENNY: Are you gonna try to be gay with me?

ELLIOT: What's that supposed to mean?

KENNY: What do you think it means, faggot?

ELLIOT: Nothing. I'm just gonna move along.

KENNY: No you're not.

ELLIOT: I'm sorry, I have to go.

KENNY: You were checking me out.

ELLIOT: What?

KENNY: You were checking me out.

ELLIOT: I think you have me confused with someone else. I have a boyfriend. I don't need to check you out.

KENNY: Where are you going?

ELLIOT: Goodnight.

KENNY: Hold on.

ELLIOT: You won't let me pass?

Elliot tries to walk by Kenny. Kenny pushes him down. Elliot tries to get up. Kenny pushes him again.

Kenny takes a metal pipe out from within his jacket and starts wailing on Elliot's head.

Elliot tries to block the pipe with his hand, but Kenny's brute force is too great.

He beats Elliot's writhing body until it is still.

Blackout.

End of Act One.

Intermission.

ACT TWO

SCENE ONE

Little B, dressed as Snow White. She's in some kid's backyard, talking to a group of 8-year-olds.

LITTLE B: Hello, my little dwarves.

> I'm Snow White.
>
> Are you whistling while you work?
>
> Are you—
>
> I'm sorry, have I said that already?
>
> Does anyone want a balloon animal?
>
> Anyone?
>
> No?
>
> What about the birthday girl?
>
> Do you want—
>
> Would the birthday girl like me to sing her a song?
>
> How about that?
>
> I'm going to sing to you.
>
> Let's see.

She begins to sing "You've Been Flirting Again" from Post:

"All that she said was true. All that she said was..."

She stops singing. Beat.

No, I know it's not from Snow White.
I don't know any of her songs.

*She begins to sing "It's Oh So Quiet"
from* Post*:*

"Shh. Shh. It's oh so quiet..."

She forgets the words, stops singing.

Um... I, um...

*She begins to sing "Human Behavior"
from* Debut*:*

"If you ever get close to a human...you'd better be ready to get confused..."

She gets lost again. Stops singing.

Um... I'm sorry.
I don't remember how any of my songs go.

My songs.

Oh my god.

I was trying to remember writing them, but I—

Excuse me, sorry, wait.

Where am I?

Right, okay.

Does anyone want a balloon animal?

Anyone?

No.

You must be thinking I'm so stupid because

'how can Snow White not know any of her own songs?'

But it's because I'm not really Snow White.

I'm not, I'm not, I'm not, I'm—

How can she not know any of her own songs?

But I'm not really—

I'm not a clown, I'm just a girl, I'm sorry.

And I'm not, I'm, I'm—

She begins singing "Bachelorette" from Homogenic:

"I'm a fountain of blood in the shape of a girl."

She stops singing.

I'm sorry.

My brother was beaten up very badly and now my head's all
mixed up.

He needs me.

I'm just trying to figure out who that is.

My parents named me Little B,

which I thought was short for Bjork,

but it's really short for Becky,

which is short for Rebecca.

And I feel really confused right now

and really. Really. Bad.

I'm sorry.

I hope you have a really good birthday.

I have to go to the hospital to be with my brother.

He needs me.

Lights fade to black.

SCENE TWO

In darkness, we hear the wail of a siren approaching. The siren's scream grows louder and louder until it's almost unbearable. Then, suddenly, the sound is sucked away, as if into a vacuum, and silence fills the air.

Lights up on Elliot in his hospital bed. Little B sits at his bedside.

Elliot wakes up.

ELLIOT: B?

LITTLE B: Elliot...

ELLIOT: Hi B, what's going on? Where am I?

LITTLE B: You're awake.

ELLIOT: Yeah. What's going on?

LITTLE B: You've been asleep for nine days.

ELLIOT: Really?

LITTLE B: I'm afraid it's all my fault. I'm sorry if it is, Elliot.

ELLIOT: What do you mean?

LITTLE B (*a rush*): If I didn't want a job, then you never would've met Caleb, which would've been terrible, but you also might not have been there that night and, oh Elliot, I'm so sorry, I'm so

116

confused, I can't even...

ELLIOT: What's going on?

LITTLE B: Everyone's here. They need to know you're awake.

(*calling off*)

Mom! Caleb! Becky! Kristen! Everyone, he's awake!

> *Mom enters, followed by Caleb, Becky*
> *and Kristen.*

MOM: Oh my god, thank God.

LITTLE B: He's awake.

ELLIOT: Why are you all looking at me like that?

MOM: Don't worry. You're safe now.

ELLIOT: Safe from what?

LITTLE B: You're awake.

MOM: Oh, honey. Honey.

ELLIOT: WILL SOMEONE TELL ME WHAT'S GOING ON?

CALEB: You're at Cedars. And you're safe now.

ELLIOT: But what. The fuck. Am I safe from?

> *Lights shift.*

SCENE THREE

Elliot lies in his hospital bed, asleep.
Becky and Kristen sit at his side.

KRISTEN: Becky?

Becky looks up at Kristen.

KRISTEN: He's gonna be okay.

BECKY: Says who?

KRISTEN: I'm reading one of the books your mom gave me for my birthday. And I played the book game with it. I found out his fortune. He's gonna be okay.

BECKY: Some book says my brother's gonna be okay?

KRISTEN: Yeah.

BECKY: That's the stupidest thing I've ever heard in my life.

KRISTEN: We agreed to be positive, here, Becky. Remember? I'm trying to be positive.

BECKY: You have it with you? The book? The book that says my brother's gonna be okay?

Kristen grabs her bag, retrieves the
book. She offers it to Becky, who takes it.

BECKY: Ask it again.

KRISTEN: Okay, so I'm thinking something in my head. It's a rule.

Do you agree to abide by the rule that I have in my head?

BECKY: What is it?

KRISTEN: Doesn't Elliot make you agree first?

BECKY: I want you to say the rule out loud. To make sure the book

knows what we're talking about. So everything's crystal clear.

KRISTEN: Okay. So the rule that I have in my head is that whatever

sentence we land on will be Elliot's fortune. To let us know if

he's going to be okay or not.

BECKY: Now tell me when to stop.

Becky flips through pages in the book.

KRISTEN: Stop.

*Becky stops. She holds the book open to
the pages she's stopped on.*

BECKY: Tell me when to stop.

*Becky alternates between the left page
and right page.*

KRISTEN: Stop.

Becky stops. She moves her finger up and down that page.

BECKY: One more time.
KRISTEN: Stop.

Becky stops. She reads the sentence her finger has landed on to herself.

KRISTEN: Is he gonna be okay?
BECKY: (*reads whatever sentence her finger has landed on. She reads the entire sentence, whatever it is.*) That doesn't make any sense.

Kristen might ad-lib a response to the sentence. If it sounds like an affirmative answer, she might remark on that. If it sounds negative or inconclusive, she might suggest trying again. But Becky shuts the book, gives it back to Kristen.

BECKY: That doesn't mean anything. I hate the book game, it doesn't mean anything.
KRISTEN: Don't take it out on me.
BECKY: I'm not taking anything out on you.
KRISTEN: If you're angry, you should be angry—
BECKY: I'm not angry.

KRISTEN: —but stop being passive aggressive.

BECKY: I'm not being passive aggressive.

KRISTEN: Fine.

Beat.

KRISTEN: This sucks. I need some good news. Tell me something good. How's the baby?

BECKY: I don't know. Rose is with him. She won't take her eyes off him. Ever since they put him in that plastic box. She just stands there at the window looking in. I hate all of those wires they put on him. He looks helpless. Like his Great Uncle Elliot. They both look so helpless.

KRISTEN: They're gonna be—

BECKY: "Okay." I know.

Beat.

KRISTEN: I forgot to tell you. I talked to Jim.

BECKY: What does that asshole want?

KRISTEN: At the end of my shift this morning, we talked.

BECKY: And?

KRISTEN: And he wants to know when you're coming back to work, but—

BECKY: I told him. I told him about Elliot. I told him about Rose. Doesn't he—

KRISTEN: He knows. That's not what we talked about. I quit, Becky.

BECKY: What?

KRISTEN: So much has happened this last week. I haven't had a chance to tell you. I found a new job. A real job.

BECKY: You're quitting?

KRISTEN: I did it. I told Jim last night. I'm not going to strip anymore. It's killing me.

BECKY: You've been stripping for, what? Eight months? And it's killing you?

KRISTEN: We said we wanted out. It's not gonna happen unless we just do it.

BECKY: I've been stripping since I was 15. What else am I supposed to do?

KRISTEN: I told Jim you weren't coming back either.

BECKY: What?

KRISTEN: You can find something. I'll cover things until then.

BECKY: What do you mean? What if I can't find anything? Why would you do that? Why would tell him I was quitting?

KRISTEN: We talked about this.

BECKY: But with all the extra hospital bills—

KRISTEN: We'll figure it out—

BECKY: We won't. We need the money—

Elliot wakes up.

KRISTEN: We'll figure it out—

BECKY: But what if we don't?

ELLIOT: Becky?

BECKY: Elliot, Elliot, hi Elliot. You're awake.

Lights shift.

SCENE FOUR

We're at The French Market. A young man, Avi, sits at a table, waiting. Mom enters.

MOM: I'm sorry I'm late.

AVI: It's okay. Are you okay?

MOM: I'm okay.

AVI: I got us a table, we're just waiting to get seated.

MOM: Thank you, Avi. Avi?

AVI: Yeah?

MOM: I was mugged.

AVI: What?

MOM: I was mugged.

AVI: Oh my God, are you okay?

MOM: I don't know.

AVI: Did you call the cops? We have to call the cops.

MOM: No, don't. Don't. I'm fine.

AVI: We have to do something. What did he take?

MOM: Nothing. I don't even know why I told you. I don't know why
    that just came out of my mouth.

AVI: Rose, what's going on? Tell me everything that happened.

MOM: It happened out in the street. It was a busy street, there were
    cars driving by. It was right by this coffee shop where some
    people were sitting and he grabbed me. Just up the sidewalk, just

down the block—there were some people there too. And they saw it happen. They saw the guy grab me—he grabbed my purse and I was holding onto it, and I fell. And I was yelling at him, you know, "fuck you, you fucking fuck," yelling. It happened so quick, it's not like anyone could have stopped him, but they saw it—I know they did. They heard me—I know they did. And I know that it happened quickly. And I know that they couldn't have done anything to stop him. But after he was gone, they could've—none of them—not a single one of them—none of them came over to help me, to help me off the ground, to see if I was all right, to call the police, nothing, nothing, no one came over.

AVI: Well, I'm gonna do something. I'm calling the cops.

MOM: No, Avi, don't—

AVI: Something has to be done.

MOM: No—this happened a couple of months ago.

AVI: What?

MOM: I never told anyone because no one needed to know. I wasn't hurt, I was fine. I didn't want them to worry. But then I think about what happened to Elliot. And I wonder if anyone saw. If anyone heard. Because they got to him pretty quick, but the guy was already gone, so they didn't get to him quick enough. What if they...? I don't even know what I'm talking about. People did get to him and thank God for that, I just...wish they'd gotten to him sooner, that's all. I'm afraid I'm going crazy, Avi. I think we should break up.

AVI: What do you mean?

MOM: My son's in the hospital. My great-grandson's too small to breathe without a machine. Everything's falling apart. And I don't want you to feel like I'm dragging you down with me. You're young—

AVI: Rose—

MOM: You have so many other things you could worry about—

AVI: Rose—

MOM: I'm just your Mrs. Robinson fling and I understand that. I do. And it's okay. But we should stop before one of us gets hurt.

AVI: Rose, I love you.

MOM: You do?

AVI: Yes. And you're not my Mrs. Robinson fling. And you can tell me anything and it won't feel like a burden. And I don't want to break up with you. I love you.

MOM: Oh thank God because I love you too and I don't want to break up with you either and I really need you right now and I'm afraid that I'm a burden because everything's falling apart so thank God that you aren't. You really don't want to break up with me?

AVI: I really don't want to break up with you.

MOM: If my son dies...If he dies before me, I'll kill myself. Why can't I protect them from the world?

AVI: He's gonna be okay. He is. And you're a good mom. You've protected them from a lot.

MOM: Shhhh....I need you—. I need you to do something for me...

AVI: Okay.

MOM: I need you to touch me.

He pulls his chair closer to hers.

MOM: Please. Right now. Please.

He touches her face. She guides his hand down, across her chest. She moves it down lower, underneath the table, in between her legs. She guides his fingers inside her.

Several beats. She leans her head back and starts crying.

Lights shift.

SCENE FIVE

The Pink Tulips strip club. A small cubicle. Becky enters, followed by Frank.

BECKY: Have a seat. Now let's do this.

> *She snaps her fingers. Some sexy-groovy-base beats begin to pump through the sound system. Becky starts swaying her hips to the beat of the bump. After a moment:*

FRANK: You're Hunter, right? I'm Frank. Don't you remember me?

BECKY (*still dancing*): Should I remember you?

FRANK: You've danced for me before.

BECKY: Have I?

FRANK: About five months ago. At Valley Ball. You don't remember?

BECKY: I do a lot of dancing, Frank.

FRANK: We did more than dance.

> *He puts his hand on her ass.*

BECKY: Well that's all I do now.

She gently removes his hand.

FRANK: You thought I—. You said—
BECKY: Shhhh.
FRANK: Do you remember what you—. What you said?

> *She continues her lap dance, doesn't reply.*

FRANK: About my—.

> *Beat.*

I was wondering if we could, um...

> *He wants to ask her out, but he can't get out the words.*

FRANK: I love you, Hunter.
BECKY: No you don't.
FRANK: I do.

> *He puts his hand on her again, tries to kiss her.*

> *Becky removes his hand again.*

BECKY: No—

FRANK: Would you hold me?

He grabs her again, more aggressively.

BECKY: Frank, stop—

FRANK: Just hold me.

BECKY (*forceful*): I told you to stop.

She stops dancing, steps away from him.

FRANK: (desperate) I tried to see him, like you told me. He wasn't
there, but I tried. I'll try again. I will. I'll go. I can change.
Doesn't that get me anywhere with you?

BECKY: Get the fuck out of here, okay?

*She stands away from him. Frank gets up
and goes.*

*A moment later, Kristen pokes her head
in.*

KRISTEN: Becky, get dressed.

BECKY: What?

KRISTEN: Rose just called, she's having the baby.

BECKY: What do you mean?

KRISTEN: Come on, let's go.

BECKY: She can't be having the baby yet, it's too soon.

KRISTEN: Well Little B just drove her to the hospital and it's
    happening, so let's go.

BECKY: I need to call my mom, I need to call Elliot.

KRISTEN: You can call them from the car, let's go, let's go.

Lights shift.

SCENE SIX

*Hospital room. Elliot's asleep. Barry sits
at his bedside.*

Elliot wakes up, looks at Barry.

ELLIOT: Who are you?

BARRY: You don't recognize me?

ELLIOT: No.

BARRY: Not even a tiny bit?

ELLIOT: I don't think so.

BARRY: We're friends.

ELLIOT: Really?

BARRY: Yeah. You're part of my circle.

ELLIOT: I have a circle?

BARRY: Of course you do. You really don't remember me?

ELLIOT: My head is so, so fucked.

BARRY: Fucked up?

ELLIOT: Yeah. Feel free...

BARRY: What do you mean?

ELLIOT: Feel free to finish my, my...

BARRY: To finish your sentences?

ELLIOT: Yeah. My head's like scrambled eggs.

BARRY: Okay.

ELLIOT: We're friends, but I don't remember your name.

BARRY: It's Barry.

ELLIOT: Barry. Some things I remember, I remember them in the wrong places. And sometimes it's like that game.

BARRY: What game?

ELLIOT: That game you play when you're a kid. I'll be, I'll be...

Beat.

A memory will come back to me, I'll be remembering something, and then my brain will, my brain will say "stop."

BARRY: Red light.

ELLIOT: Right. And I have to go back. Until my brain says...

BARRY: Green Light.

ELLIOT: Right. I have to go back and try to, to, to remember from the beginning again. Do you, do you remember how we met? Sometimes details, you know...

BARRY: Sometimes details help?

ELLIOT: Yeah. So how did we...

BARRY: We're neighbors. There was a barbecue. A mixer, for the apartment building. That's where we met.

ELLIOT: Did we fight about a piece of chicken?

BARRY: No.

ELLIOT: I remember fighting with someone...

BARRY: About a piece of chicken?

ELLIOT: Yeah.

BARRY: No, we never fought about chicken. When we met, our first conversation was about Caleb. You'd just started dating him and you were excited because you thought it might be the real—

ELLIOT (*remembering*): The real deal.

BARRY: That's what you said.

ELLIOT: You know Caleb?

BARRY: We've met. He's a good guy, I like him.

ELLIOT: Me too.

BARRY: Yeah, well, he loves you, I can tell. And I think you were right. I think he's the real deal. You know, he never leaves the hospital.

ELLIOT: Really?

BARRY: Well, occasionally. He's at a birthday party right now. But he's here a lot. You know, I always say "make the most of what God gave you." The way I look at it, you're a lucky guy, because even though you're sitting here in the hospital, God gave you Caleb. It evens out somewhere.

ELLIOT: Wait.

BARRY: What?

ELLIOT: I just remembered, you and I... Did we...?

BARRY: Did we fuck?

ELLIOT: Yeah.

BARRY: No, you and I, we never fucked. Two guys that looked exactly like us, they fucked a little bit. But then at Ted's barbecue, you said you wanted to start over. So we started over. Clean slate.

ELLIOT: So Caleb doesn't...

BARRY: He doesn't know. He just knows that you're part of my circle.

ELLIOT: I always wanted a circle.

BARRY: Yeah, me too.

Lights shift.

SCENE SEVEN

Little B and Caleb sit on a park bench.
Caleb wears his clown costume, Little B
is in her Snow White outfit. Caleb holds
his wig in his lap. Little B still wears
hers.

CALEB: How are you, Little B?

LITTLE B: I don't know. How are you, Bobo?

CALEB: I'm sad.

LITTLE B: Yeah, me too.

CALEB: Have you been to see him yet today?

LITTLE B: Yeah.

CALEB: How was he?

LITTLE B: A little bit better. He seems to be remembering more every
    day. He doesn't remember what happened to him yet.

CALEB: I'm gonna be there tonight.

LITTLE B: Good.

(*urgent*)

I need to talk to you.

CALEB: What?

LITTLE B: I think I'm different.

CALEB: What do you mean?

LITTLE B: I've been remembering things. Painful things. About this person I used to be. Before I was so internationally renowned and eccentric.

Beat. It's hard for B to talk about this.

I always really liked Bjork. She was always my favorite.

CALEB: So you're not her anymore?

LITTLE B: I guess not. I don't know. I don't know who I am. I'm scared.

CALEB: It's okay. It's good.

LITTLE B: You're the first person I've told. Do you think that everyone's going to be mad at me?

CALEB: I think they're gonna be happy. That you're yourself again.

LITTLE B: I don't even know how to tell them. I don't even know how to talk to them.

CALEB: You just talk.

Beat.

CALEB: How long have you known, B?

LITTLE B: I started to suspect about five months ago, after my dad died. Then when Elliot got beaten up...it just came to me.

Beat.

137

LITTLE B: Is there anything new with the police. Have they found the guy?

CALEB: No. They're not really looking.

LITTLE B: Why not?

CALEB: If Elliot could remember what the guy looked like, then they'd have a lead. But they don't have anything to go on.

Beat.

LITTLE B: Bobo?

CALEB: What?

LITTLE B: I'm sorry, I mean Caleb.

CALEB: It's okay. You can call me Bobo.

LITTLE B: Only if you want me to.

CALEB: I want you to.

LITTLE B: I just...I don't think I can work for you anymore.

CALEB: Why not?

LITTLE B: I just think, for a while at least, I don't want to be anyone other than who I am.

CALEB: Okay.

LITTLE B: Does everyone think I'm weird? People must think I'm a freak.

CALEB: People who don't know you.

LITTLE B: Don't tell anyone about what we talked about, okay?

CALEB: No, you should do it.

LITTLE B: Yeah. I will.

Little B takes off her wig.

LITTLE B: I'm gonna do it.

Beat.

LITTLE B: I'm glad we had this talk.

CALEB: Yeah, me too.

LITTLE B: Give Elliot a kiss for me, when you see him tonight.

CALEB: I will.

LITTLE B: And you can have this back.

She hands him the wig.

LITTLE B: See you later.

Caleb gives her a little wave, watches as she walks off. He sits there with the two wigs for a moment, lost in thought.

Lights shift.

SCENE EIGHT

The high school parking lot. 10 p.m.

Frank stands underneath a street lamp, waiting.

Damien walks by, his head buried in his Midsummer *script, memorizing lines. He almost doesn't notice Frank standing there. But then:*

FRANK: Hey.

Damien stops, looks at Frank.

FRANK: How's it going?
DAMIEN: Fine.
FRANK: I just...wanted to see you, and..., um...
DAMIEN: What do you want?
FRANK: I just wanted to see how you were doing.

Damien shrugs.

FRANK: You have every reason to hate me.

Beat. Damien just stands there.

FRANK: I hear you're doing a play.

DAMIEN: You don't have to pretend you're interested.

FRANK: I am interested.

DAMIEN: It's just really weird to see you in the school parking lot.

FRANK: I know, I'm sorry.

DAMIEN: At ten p.m.

FRANK: Your mom said you were in rehearsal.

DAMIEN: So she, like, sent you here?

FRANK: No. She didn't think you'd want to see me.

DAMIEN: It's just kind of creepy.

FRANK: But I wanted to see you.

DAMIEN: Why?

FRANK: You're my son. I want to know how you're doing.

DAMIEN: Since when?

FRANK: I know it's been awhile, but I—

DAMIEN: It's been a year.

FRANK: I'm sorry.

DAMIEN: You can't just stand in a parking lot and say that you're
    sorry.

FRANK: But I am. I want to try harder.

DAMIEN: That's what you said a year ago.

FRANK: I'm trying.

DAMIEN: Why?

FRANK: Because I love you.

DAMIEN: You're such a fucking asshole, do you know that?

FRANK: Yeah, I know.

DAMIEN: So that's all?

FRANK: What do you mean?

DAMIEN: You're sorry and you love me?

FRANK: Yeah.

Beat. Damien doesn't say anything.

FRANK: What's the play?

DAMIEN: What?

FRANK: That you're doing. What is it?

DAMIEN: *A Midsummer Night's Dream.*

FRANK: Who are you playing?

DAMIEN: Puck.

FRANK: He's the fairy, right?

DAMIEN: Yeah.

FRANK: Be careful. Monkey see, monkey do.

DAMIEN: I guess.

FRANK: That's a good part for you, though. He's funny. You can be funny. When are the performances?

DAMIEN: It's just one weekend.

FRANK: When?

DAMIEN: Two weeks from this Friday.

FRANK: Can I come?

DAMIEN: I don't care. You can do whatever you want. You already
do.

FRANK: I want to come.

DAMIEN: I'll believe it when I see it.

FRANK: How are you getting home? Do you need a ride?

DAMIEN: I have a car.

FRANK: Since when?

DAMIEN: Since I worked all summer.

FRANK: That's your car over there?

DAMIEN: Yeah.

FRANK: What happened to the paint?

DAMIEN: This girl...

*Damien shakes his head. He doesn't
want to go there.*

FRANK: Okay, well. I'll see you at your play. Maybe we could go to
Denny's afterwards? Get dessert. Unless you have plans with
your friends...

DAMIEN: We could do that.

FRANK: Really?

DAMIEN: If you actually come.

FRANK: I will.

DAMIEN: Dad, you say things like that, and then you don't. I mean, if
you're not gonna come through again, it'd be better if you just
stopped trying. Like, stop trying now, you know? Because you

shouldn't start something you can't finish. Does that make sense? I've thought about this a lot, you know? And if you really want to see me in the play, then you should come. But if you're just doing it because you, like, feel bad about yourself...and seeing the play will make you feel better, but then you won't try as hard because you'll feel like that's enough for awhile...? If that's what you're gonna do, just don't do it, okay? Do you understand what I'm saying?

Frank nods. He can't speak.

Damien exits.

Frank watches as his son gets into his car, drives away.

Lights shift.

SCENE NINE

The neonatal ICU at the hospital. Becky stands outside, looking through the window at her grandson. Kristen approaches.

KRISTEN: How is he?

BECKY: He's sleeping. The doctor said we can take him home tomorrow.

KRISTEN: That's great. Does Rose know?

BECKY: Yeah. She went home to take a nap.

KRISTEN: They're releasing Elliot too. I was just down there.

BECKY: They are?

KRISTEN: Yeah. We're gonna be all right. Everyone's gonna be okay.

Kristen puts her arms around Becky, who flinches and moves away.

KRISTEN: What's wrong?

BECKY: I just don't want you to touch me. In public.

KRISTEN: I'm your girlfriend.

BECKY: I feel uncomfortable.

KRISTEN: You don't want people to know we're together?

BECKY: I don't feel safe right now. I don't feel comfortable, okay?

145

KRISTEN: So tomorrow, when you and Rose bring the baby home—
do you want me there, so we can be together as a family? Or do
you want me to stay at home so no one at the hospital has to
know we're actually a couple?

BECKY: I want you there. I need you there for Rose.

Beat.

I don't think I'm going to be there.

KRISTEN: What do you mean? Where are you gonna be?

BECKY: I don't know.

KRISTEN: Becky—

*Kristen reaches for Becky, who flinches
again.*

BECKY: Don't touch me. Stop it, okay? Just stop it. I don't want you
to touch me. I need some space, okay. Please. I'm sorry. I love
you. But I'm about to crawl out of my skin. Elliot's okay. And
my grandson's okay. So now I'm gonna go. I just need to
disappear, okay? I need to get away from you, and my family,
and the club—I just need to get away from everything.

KRISTEN: Where are you going?

BECKY: I don't want to talk. I don't want you to try to stop me. I
don't want you to say anything that will make this harder than it
is. I don't know where I'm going. I don't know if I'm coming

back. I just need to figure out a lot of things. I don't expect you to understand. But would you tell Rose that I love her? And would you tell the rest of the family that I'm sorry for running away again? And would you tell Little B I wish I could be a better big sister? And tell Mom it's not about her. And tell Elliot that I hope he understands that I love him, that this isn't about him, and I waited until I knew he was gonna be okay. And if Rose starts to forget that I love her, would you tell her I love her again? And, just—could you do all that? I love you too. I love you too. And I hope that someday you can still love me. I just—I don't want to be touched. I've been touched my whole life. And I can't—I just don't want to be touched anymore. So...

> *Becky exits. Kristen stands there alone for a beat. Lights shift.*

SCENE TEN

Elliot and Caleb are on the street corner in West Hollywood outside "Heaven," the dance club.

It's mid-afternoon. The neon sign that says "Heaven" hasn't yet been turned on.

ELLIOT: 'I love you.' Um, um.

CALEB: It's okay. If you wanna—

ELLIOT: No.

CALEB: —stop.

ELLIOT: 'I love you so much it, it, it. It.'

CALEB: It's okay.

ELLIOT: 'It kind of freaks me out.'

CALEB: And then we kissed.

They kiss.

CALEB: And then you said you needed to tell me something.

ELLIOT: That's right. 'I need to tell you something.'

CALEB: And then I said, 'Wait.'

ELLIOT: What?

CALEB: Exactly, that's what you said. 'What?'

148

ELLIOT: 'What?'

CALEB: 'I forgot my jacket.'

ELLIOT: 'No, wait, let me—'

CALEB: 'Hold on. I'll be right back.' And then I ran inside.

ELLIOT: Go.

CALEB: You're sure?

ELLIOT: Yeah, go.

> *Elliot watches Caleb run back into the club.*

> *Now he's alone again. He stands there, still, trying to remember the attack. We can see in his eyes how terrifying it is to be alone here. The longer Caleb is gone, the scarier it gets.*

> *A total of two minutes and thirty-seven seconds pass. Finally, Caleb returns.*

CALEB: And then I came back.

ELLIOT: That's how, how, how long you were gone?

CALEB: Two minutes, thirty-seven seconds. I know because the call timer in your cell phone was still running from Becky's call.

ELLIOT: I still don't remember the rest.

CALEB: When I came back I was holding my jacket. The guy was already gone, I never saw him. And you, you were on the ground. There. You weren't moving. I thought you were...

Beat.

Um, and I went down to the ground and kind of...lifted you up. Into my arms. You were bleeding, you know? And I couldn't quite tell where all of it was coming from. But your eyes were open and you were still breathing and I started shouting for help. Everything else happened really fast. The ambulance, the hospital. Your family was already there, for Rose. She was on the third floor, still in labor. You were on the first. I stayed in the Emergency waiting room. As close to you as I could get. Your mom and Little B were there most of the time, with me. Becky and Kristen were going back and forth all night.

ELLIOT: I still don't remember.

CALEB: What were you going to tell me?

ELLIOT: When?

CALEB: That night? Do you know?

ELLIOT: Do you, do, do you love me?

CALEB: Yes.

ELLIOT: And you're never gonna leave, leave—

CALEB: No.

ELLIOT: You're never gonna leave me?

CALEB: If I was gonna go, I'd be gone by now. You're stuck with me.

ELLIOT: Even if what I tell you isn't, isn't—

CALEB: I can handle it.

ELLIOT: If it isn't good.

CALEB: Trust me.

ELLIOT: I remember. I remember what I was going to tell you. I, I, I, I, I, I don't know how to say it, exactly. My words aren't great anyway. You're the best. You're the best thing that's ever, that's ever happened to me and I've never really had a best thing before so I, I, I, I, I, I, I, I, I don't want to fuck it, fuck it up but I'm afraid that, I'm afraid that what I'm going to tell you is going to fuck it up because I kind of fucked it, up. I don't even know how to say it. I still, I feel, I feel awkward with the words. I'll just say it. I'll just. I'll just. I'll just say it. You know that I love you. I love you. So I had sex with this guy while we were dating, it was before you asked me to be your boyfriend, but we'd already been on a few dates. He lives in, he lives in my place, not my place, my building; I paid him for it. For the, for the. I kind of have— used to have—a problem with paying people for it. I went to his apartment and he fucked me, he fucked me, he fucked me, and I didn't tell you about it and I'm, I'm, I'm, I'm, I'm sorry I did it. And I did it, I did it, I did it because I love you and because I'm afraid of, I'm afraid of, of, of losing you. And I know that sounds weird and weak, but this freaks me out. To love you so, so, so, so, so, so, so, so, so, so—. So much. I have problems. I've been messed up for a long time. Things happened when I was a kid, I was abused for a long, for a long, for a long time and I don't

151

really know how to be healthy. You make me feel healthy.
You're the best thing that's ever happened to me. I've never had
a best thing. I told you that. I've never really had one, I've never.
And you should know that I'm, that I'm, I'm fucked up. Like,
I'm fucked up in the head now, but I've always been kind of
fucked up in the heart.

CALEB: You're not.

ELLIOT: I am. But it's okay. Because you still love me, right?

CALEB: Yeah, I do.

ELLIOT: Will you marry me someday?

CALEB: I was gonna ask you that.

ELLIOT: You were? Okay, then...

They kiss.

Lights shift.

152

SCENE ELEVEN

Kristen and Rose enter their living room.
Rose holds her new baby.

KRISTEN: Here we are.

ROSE: Home.

KRISTEN: I can't believe he's still sleeping. He's such a good boy.

ROSE: Yeah.

KRISTEN: She'll be back, Rose. She loves you. She'll be back.

ROSE: Where did she go?

KRISTEN: That's what she wanted me to tell you—that she loves you.

ROSE: But where did she go?

KRISTEN: I don't know. I don't know.

ROSE: You're not going to leave me too, are you?

KRISTEN: No.

ROSE: You promise?

KRISTEN: You're my family. I can't imagine leaving this. Listen, I'm gonna go see what's in the kitchen. We'll talk about this over dinner, okay?

ROSE: Okay.

Kristen exits.

ROSE (*to her baby*): I need to talk to you. Like an adult. I'm really freaked out right now. Life is, like, so fucked up in so many ways, and it's also really good and I want you to know that. There are so many things I want to tell you. First, do you remember those twins that were born a week after you? They were with you for a couple of days, then their mom got to take them home, but I talked to their mom and she taught me something. See, she already had a three-year-old, and her little three-year-old girl was the most talkative person I've ever met in my entire life. Seriously. I swear to God. She was so smart. And she used all of these, like, enormous words for a three-year-old. For instance, I asked her if she was happy about having two new brothers and she said, "actually, they make me nervous." She actually used the word 'actually.' And I asked her why her brothers made her nervous, and she said, "because they're so small. I thought I'd be able to play with them immediately, but if I do, I'll break them." Can you believe that? This was a three-year-old talking. And I asked her mother if she did anything special; like, what kind of cereal did she eat, or what kind of bedtime stories did she read. Like, what secret did she know to make her daughter so smart? And this mother looked at me and she said, "I never said the words ga-ga or goo-goo. I never talked down to her." It's such a simple thing, it's almost too simple. But it's brilliant, right? So that's what I'm going to do with you. And you're going to be so smart. And you're going to be the best thing that's ever happened to this family, I just know it.

Beat. Rose looks around.

154

So, look around: this is your home.

Beat.

And I'm your mom. My name's Rose. I was named after my grandmother, your great-grandmother Rose. I think it's supposed to be blasphemous to name someone after someone who's still alive, but my mom ran away from home when she was pregnant with me and so it all kind of works out. 'Cause she didn't want to forget her mom. That's how I see it, anyway. My mom and I have never really talked about it. I mean, I've tried to talk to her about it, but whenever I do, mom'll say something like she's trying to live in the present. I don't push her too much because I know she'd offer more information if she was ready to. I don't know if you'll ever meet her, but while you were in the hospital she spent a lot of time watching you. She'd stand at the glass with me and we'd both watch you together. So that must mean something. It must mean that she loves you. I have to stop talking about her right now because I just don't understand how she could leave this and I'm really fucking mad. You can't say fuck until you're eighteen, okay? So don't listen to me when I say it.

Beat.

Your Great Uncle Elliot gave me this present recently. It was his journal, from when he was a kid. I guess the word 'kid' is relative, because he was my age. I'm not a kid, I'm a mom. You're a kid. So frick'n weird. Anyway, he gave me this journal a few weeks ago, so I had a lot of time to read it while I was waiting to bring you home from intensive care. That place was kind of scary, wasn't it? I hated it. That incubator you had to be in? Weren't those wires awful? I wanted to pick you up so badly it hurt.

Beat.

Look at you, you're so good.

Beat, as she rocks her baby for a moment.

Anyway, as I was saying before, this journal of Elliot's, it was hard to read. My mom and him, and then later Aunt B—they didn't have a good childhood. Their dad was not a good man. That's all you need to know for now. Just that he wasn't good. And I'm not talking down to you by not telling you exactly what went down. Just protecting you. That's all I want to say about that for now.

Beat.

And your dad? He's not a bad man. He's an asshole, but he's not a bad man. There's a difference. Maybe he'll be a part of your life someday, maybe he won't. But regardless, there's so much love in our family for you right now, and you're barely seven pounds, imagine when you start having a personality. You're living proof that this family keeps getting better with every generation. I love you, Little D.

She begins to sing to her baby, to the tune of Bjork's Cocoon.

ROSE: *How could I have known*
   That a boy like you
   Would change me so completely
   Perfecting our family?
   How could I have known
   That a boy like you
   Would make all my dreams
   Come true so suddenly?

Fade to black.

END OF PLAY

About the Playwright

ERIK PATTERSON is an award-winning playwright, screenwriter, and writing teacher.

His play, *One of the Nice Ones*, earned the Los Angeles Drama Critics Circle Award. His theater work has been produced or developed by Playwrights' Arena, the Los Angeles Theatre Centre, Theatre of NOTE, the Evidence Room, The Actors' Gang, the Echo Theater Company, the Lark Play Development Center, Moving Arts, Black Dahlia, Naked Angels, the Mark Taper Forum, and New Group. His plays have been nominated for the Ovation Award, the Stage Raw Award, the LA Weekly Award, and the GLAAD Media Award.

His writing for TV has been recognized with the Humanitas Prize and the Writer's Guild Award, as well as two Emmy nominations. Along with his writing partner, Jessica Scott, Erik has written films for Warner Bros., Universal, 20th Century Fox, Disney, Freeform, MTV, Paramount, Hallmark, and Syfy, among others. Film and TV credits include: *Abandoned* (starring Emma Roberts and Michael Shannon), *R.L. Stine's The Haunting Hour*, *Another Cinderella Story* (starring Selena Gomez and Jane Lynch), *Deep Blue Sea 2*, *Radio Rebel*, and many more.

Erik is a graduate of Occidental College and the British American Drama Academy. He hosts a gently-guided writing sprint online called "Sunday Sprints" that attracts writers seeking community and inspiration to do their best work.

www.erikpatterson.org

Plays by Erik Patterson

Tonseisha

drama / 1 female, 5 male / 45 minutes, no intermission

A young Japanese woman is haunted by the loss of two men: her father, whom she barely knew, and cult novelist Richard Brautigan, whom she never met. Akiko plays out her father/Richard Brautigan fantasies with a new man nearly every night. Each one of her relationships begins in a bar and ends in a bedroom, and she's never satisfied. She's so lost...can she ever be found?

Yellow Flesh / Alabaster Rose

dark comedy / 5 female, 4 male / full length, one intermission

Elliot is lost in a world of sex workers—late night house calls from hustlers and phone calls with call girls. Becky is torn between two worlds—her day job as a stripper and being a mom to fifteen-year-old Rose (a Goth girl who wants nothing to do with her). And then there's Little B, who has stripped away every piece of herself until all she has left is her obsession with Icelandic pop singer Bjork. This troubled family's shared past holds unspeakable horrors and they must join forces if they ever want to heal. *Winner of the Backstage West Garland Award for Best Playwriting.*

Red Light, Green Light

drama / 6 female, 7 male / full length, one intermission

A gay clown. Two lesbian strippers. A pregnant Goth teen. A deadbeat dad. A horny mother. And a girl who thinks she's Bjork. In this stand-alone sequel to *Yellow Flesh / Alabaster Rose*, the Silverstein family journey towards healing is abruptly halted when Elliot becomes the victim of a brutal gay bashing.

He Asked For It

drama / 1 female, 6 male / full length, one intermission

It's the early 2000s, before PrEP. Ted is new to Los Angeles, and newly out of the closet. He goes on a journey through Hollywood back rooms, nightclub bathrooms, and Internet chat rooms—where he meets and falls in love with Henry. But Henry doesn't yet know how to navigate the dating landscape with his new HIV diagnosis, so he breaks things off with Ted...who then makes a desperate decision to win Henry back. *He Asked For It* asks how far are you willing to go for love? And how much will you forgive? *GLAAD Media Award nominee for Outstanding Los Angeles Theater.*

Sick

dramedy / 3 female, 3 male, 1 child / full length, no intermission
David needs to get laid, Gary could use a drink, and Tim would like you to take your top off. Carla craves cocaine, Jeannie's got God, and Pamela keeps digging herself deeper into the funny and frightening world of hypochondria. But when one of their own gets sick for real, they're all going to have to face their greatest fears and grow up.

I Wanna Hold Your Hand

dramedy / 3 female, 3 male / full length, no intermission
Our lives can change in an instant. One moment you're getting engaged, and a few surreal moments later you're sitting with strangers in an ICU waiting room, praying your fiancé will survive a brain aneurysm. While waiting for Frank to wake from a coma, Ada meets Julia, Paul, and Josh, who are waiting for their mom to wake up. A tenuous friendship is born. *I Wanna Hold Your Hand* looks at life, death, and recovery, and what it means to try your hand at living again...

One of the Nice Ones

dark comedy / 2 female, 2 male / 90 minutes, no intermission
A paraplegic woman plays outrageous power games to get something she desperately wants in this dark, twisty, sexy play that takes office politics to new extremes. *Winner of the Los Angeles Drama Critics Circle Award for Best Playwriting.*

Handjob

dark comedy / 2 female, 4 male / 90 minutes, no intermission
An encounter between a white, gay playwright and his black, straight "shirtless maid" goes disastrously wrong when signals are misinterpreted, lines crossed. *Handjob* explores the aftermath of their meeting, as it reveals deep layers of discrimination, discord, and discontent among people who should be allies. How do you know when you've gone too far if you completely ignore other people's boundaries?

Books by Erik Patterson

Pop Prompts: 200 Writing Prompts Inspired by Popular Music
Available in paperback and e-book

Pop Prompts is a collection of writing prompts that will help you dig deeper and break through creative blocks. Each prompt is paired with a pop song. Let the music be your muse as you work on your memoir, novel, script, poem—or even your own songs. This book can also be a daily jumpstart for therapeutic journaling. Use it however you want, whenever you want. As long as you're writing you're doing it right.

Pop Prompts For Swifties: 99 Writing Prompts
Available in paperback and e-book

Every writing prompt in this book is paired with one of Taylor's songs from the first "era" of her storytelling journey, from her debut album *Taylor Swift* (2006), to *Fearless* (2008), to *Speak Now* (2010), to *Red* (2012), and all the way through *1989* (2014). You don't even have to be a Swiftie—anyone can use these prompts for self-expression and reflection. As a bonus, each prompt includes blank journal pages. Inspiration is only a song away. Put on your favorite Taylor Swift album, pick a prompt, and start writing! Taylor Swift has no involvement in this book. The use of her name is merely descriptive and should not be interpreted as a sign of endorsement.

SUNDAY SPRINTS

Need some motivation?

Do you work better when someone is holding you accountable?

Come to SUNDAY SPRINTS.

Erik Patterson hosts gently-guided writing sprints on Zoom every Wednesday from 6 to 8 p.m. PST and every Sunday from noon to 2 p.m. PST. (Yes, it's called Sunday Sprints on Wednesdays because... why not?)

Here's how it works: I give a new writing prompt every fifteen minutes. You write. That's it.

All sprinters stay on mute. Alone but not alone, you can draw creative energy from the community of writers on your screen. This is a fun, low-pressure environment—a safe space for you to experiment with your writing. No worries: I will never ask you to share your work.

You decide how to use this distraction-free writing time. Work on that screenplay, novel, short story, play, poem, song. Do some therapeutic journaling. Write letters to loved ones. Do some technical writing. Create a D&D campaign. Finish your homework. Seriously, whatever you need to work on.

Let's get that writing done. Together.

Join the Sunday Sprints Patreon at:
www.patreon.com/erikpatterson

Subscribe to the Sunday Sprints mailing list at:
www.erikpatterson.org/sundaysprints

www.ingramcontent.com/pod-product-compliance
Lightning Source LLC
Chambersburg PA
CBHW070709130626
46553CB00005B/1906